T0386103

Managing Quality

Ned Hamson and Amy Zuckerman

- Fast track route to mastering quality management

- Covers the key areas of quality management, from understanding the vital connections between customers and ISO 9000-2000 to the key steps to develop a practical, performance enhancing quality management process

- Examples and lessons from some of the world's most successful businesses, including Toyota, Solectron Technology, Sun Microsystems, Sundaram-Clayton, and Prudential Assurance Company, and ideas from the smartest thinkers, including W. Edwards Deming, Philip Crosby, Genichi Taguchi, Shigeo Shingo, and Dr. A.V. Feigenbaum

- Includes a glossary of key concepts and a comprehensive resources guide

OPERATIONS

06.07

essential management thinking at your fingertips

The right of Ned Hamson and Amy Zuckerman to be identified as the authors
of this work has been asserted in accordance with the Copyright, Designs and
Patents Act 1988

First published 2002 by
Capstone Publishing (a Wiley company)
8 Newtec Place
Magdalen Road
Oxford OX4 1RE
United Kingdom
http://www.capstoneideas.com

CIP catalogue records for this book are available from the British Library and the
US Library of Congress

ISBN 1-84112-221-1

This book is printed on acid-free paper

Substantial discounts on bulk quantities of Capstone books are available
to corporations, professional associations and other organizations. Please
contact Capstone for more details on +44 (0)1865 798 623 or (fax) +44
(0)1865 240 941 or (e-mail) info@wiley-capstone.co.uk

FSC
Mixed Sources
Product group from well-managed
forests and other controlled sources

Cert no. SGS-COC-2953
www.fsc.org
© 1996 Forest Stewardship Council

Contents

Introduction to ExpressExec

ExpressExec is 3 million words of the latest management thinking compiled into 10 modules. Each module contains 10 individual titles forming a comprehensive resource of current business practice written by leading practitioners in their field. From brand management to balanced scorecard, ExpressExec enables you to grasp the key concepts behind each subject and implement the theory immediately. Each of the 100 titles is available in print and electronic formats.

Through the ExpressExec.com Website you will discover that you can access the complete resource in a number of ways:

» printed books or e-books;
» e-content – PDF or XML (for licensed syndication) adding value to an intranet or Internet site;
» a corporate e-learning/knowledge management solution providing a cost-effective platform for developing skills and sharing knowledge within an organization;
» bespoke delivery – tailored solutions to solve your need.

Why not visit www.expressexec.com and register for free key management briefings, a monthly newsletter and interactive skills checklists. Share your ideas about ExpressExec and your thoughts about business today.

Please contact elound@wiley-capstone.co.uk for more information.

06.07.01

Quality Matters

» Quality matters because your customers want the same quality that you expect as a customer
» Different tastes and quality
» Quality in one product drives expectations for quality in another
» Quality in the business-to-business sector

Quality matters because your customers want the same quality that you expect as a customer. You know that quality is an important issue from personal experience and interest – correct? You want and expect quality healthcare, quality education for your children, and quality food, housing, and transportation for yourself and your family. In fact, you probably would agree that, in general, you want the highest quality available for any service or product you choose to purchase – at a price you can afford or choose to allocate toward that purchase.

So, perhaps the questions to begin with are:

"If you purchase a product or service that does not fully meet your basic expectations or requirements and you later determine that a higher quality product or service is available at substantially the same price, are you likely to purchase the lower quality product or service a second time?"

and

"Do you expect and require the same quality each time you purchase the same product or service? Do you believe or think that present or prospective customers or clients of your organization have basic quality expectations or requirements that differ greatly from yours?"

"Not fair," you say; "there are times when less than the best or highest quality will do ... and you take what's available without making quality the first criteria!" That is true. When pressed for time and you want/need a cup of coffee or tea, you may buy and consume the first you find. But, if it is less than satisfactory, will you or will you not look for an alternative the next time you are similarly pressed for time, or simply forego that bad cup?

So, we are agreed that consistent quality is important to the well-being of your company or organization.

DIFFERENT TASTES AND QUALITY

"But wait," you say, "there are differences in quality, are there not? Take that coffee or tea, for example. People have different tastes and sometimes they want something new or different and still expect high quality, don't they?''

You hit that one for sure. These two facts of quality alone drive more producers of products or service providers over the edge than many other business concerns. Yes, the different tastes of consumers and their desire, or need, for new or different services and products mean that assuring consistent quality is not sufficient to stay in business. It means that you must be continuously improving your current processes and then doing the same for the new products and services developed to meet your customer's or client's changing needs and expectations.

QUALITY IN ONE PRODUCT DRIVES EXPECTATIONS FOR QUALITY IN ANOTHER

Someone out there is heaving a sigh of relief just now. He's saying to himself: ''I have few competitors and there has been little change expected or required for my product in years and years. So I am off the hook, I only need to provide consistent quality.'' Well, maybe. Consider, however, the following interesting aspect of your quality expectations. When you see rising quality, greater choice in style and function, and at the same price levels or at prices lower than before for cell phones and computers, or for home appliances, how long is it before you expect the same in all your purchases? At the very least, you begin to search for those alternatives and will turn to them when found.

QUALITY IN THE BUSINESS-TO-BUSINESS SECTOR

And finally, if your organization is involved to any degree in business-to-business commerce, you ''have'' to have a quality management system in place, or soon will have to. The reason is that the majority of firms at the head of large supply chains in the automotive, aerospace, telecommunications, finance, and medical devices industries are requiring that, or at least strongly encouraging that, all current and potential suppliers be certified as meeting the quality management standards laid out by ISO 9000:2000 or its industry-specific derivative.

WHAT IS ISO 9000 AND WHY IS IT SO IMPORTANT TODAY AND FOR THE FUTURE?

ISO 9000 is the first-ever international quality standard designed for all industries worldwide, as well as the service sector. First published in 1987 by the Geneva, Switzerland-based International Organization for Standardization (ISO), ISO 9000 combines total quality management (TQM) communication and motivation techniques with documentation. It was developed as an aid to the then emerging global economy by offering companies from Vietnam to Canada, Israel to Mozambique, a quality seal of approval.

THREE KEY REASONS TO CONSIDER ISO 9000[1]

Hundreds of thousands of companies worldwide have jumped onto the ISO 9000 bandwagon for three key reasons:

1 to meet customer pressure or even mandate;
2 to improve their base quality systems – meaning how quality is tracked, measured, and approved;
3 for marketing purposes.

The latest figures on ISO 9000 certificates earned worldwide come from late December 1999. According to ISO – which now maintains an official tally of ISO 9000 certificate holders – 343,643 ISO 9000 certificates were awarded to companies in 150 countries at that time. This represented an increase of 71,796 or 26.40 percent from late 1998, which offers an indication of the continued popularity of the "standards series."

Slightly more than half of the ISO 9000 certificate holders are Europeans and growth in that region is continuous. The Far East and North America are also noted for supporting ISO 9000 efforts. Companies report that they maintain ISO 9000 efforts, despite the cost of registration, for the three reasons listed above. If ISO 9000 has survived this long and continues to be useful, it's because many large corporations have incorporated its principles into their own quality systems and because they insist that suppliers do the same.

But, by and large, the need to provide a quality seal of approval is just as important in the new millennium as it was at the end of the twentieth century. As long as companies and institutions need to offer assurance to customers and the public, and as long as major corporations and even some governments require ISO 9000 as a ticket to doing business, the standards series will remain an important process for all companies to consider.[1]

Now, we should have about everyone accounted for, yes? Even government or not-for-profit organizations can be replaced or shut down, if the quality they provide drops to levels unacceptable to the general public.

So, why should we read this book on quality and quality management systems? The definitions of quality and quality management systems or processes are legion, to say the least. Each of the thousands of books on quality published in the past 20 years has an explanation of why quality is important, a definition of what the author says it is and how the author says quality is to be achieved in processes, products, and services. How is this one different?

First, we offer views, experiences, tips, and examples based on our working knowledge of more than 1000 authors and companies from around the world. Hamson alone has worked with more than 1000 authors (people in organizations as well as consultants and researchers) and their experiences with more than 1000 companies over the past 15 years. Amy Zuckerman has viewed the work and experience of that many, at least, in her 15+ years of interviewing, researching, and writing both standard-setting books and hundreds of articles on quality standards and practices around the world.

Second, with that joint experience our bias is toward finding the most practical processes and methods that will fit the needs of organizations that want to spend neither more nor less in time, funds, and energy than is necessary to create and/or sustain an effective and efficient quality system.

Third, since the ISO 9000:2000 quality management system is quickly becoming a basic requirement for being involved in business-to-business commerce, each chapter will include the impact of the ISO system on the issues covered in the chapter, or at least how the ISO system relates to those issues.

This means that instead of exhausting you, the reader, with all possible answers and resources, we will, to the best of our ability and experience, cut through the massive information glut on quality and give you a practical and concise quality book on quality. And we will relate the ISO 9000:2000 standards to each aspect of quality management.

NOTES

1 Material is adapted from *ISO 9000 MADE EASY: A Cost-Saving Guide to Documentation and Registration* by Amy Zuckerman, formerly AMACOM Books and now published by A–Z International Associates, Amherst, MA.

What is Quality and Quality Management?

» Defining "your" quality
» What is the most basic way to determine your quality requirements?
» How do you achieve, manage, or improve quality?
  » Philip B. Crosby's approach
  » W. Edwards Deming's approach
» What is quality documentation and how does it fit into the larger picture?

Quality and love share two characteristics that cause many people to throw up their hands in despair when it comes to defining either term or applying either in everyday living. Everyone agrees that both are basic to the relationships they influence: between customer and provider (quality) and between two people who are attracted to each other. But defining what either exactly means at any given time and circumstance is where the difficulty begins. We will leave defining love to others and here will focus on the vital few, the most usable, practical and value-adding definition attached to quality.

Quality has both technical and social or human aspects to it. The technical aspects of quality most commonly refer to such items as durability, safety, and fit and finish. The social or human aspects of quality are often those that make it most difficult to define and meet over time. The customer often gives his or her requirements as if they were one stream of consciousness statement: "I want it to be the newest, high quality, at low or reasonable cost, user and earth friendly, with style and beauty, and safe. And I want it my way, at the time and place I want it!" Now, not all of those characteristics will apply to every product or service, but any supplier who does not take them into account as measures that might turn into a basic quality requirement will soon run into difficulty in today's and tomorrow's market.

DEFINING "YOUR" QUALITY

If we assume that you know what characteristics your product or service will be measured against, where do you start in defining "your" quality?

Phil Crosby gives us the most usable and generic definition of quality: "quality is conformance to requirements." Why is this such a practical and usable definition? It is the standard(s) you must aim for and achieve whether the requirements are those set by:

1 design engineers;
2 internal or external (end-use) customers;
3 government agencies;
4 national or international standard-setting bodies; or

5 industry association or consortium standard- or protocol-setting bodies.

PHILIP B. CROSBY

Philip B. Crosby, a quality advocate made famous in 1979 by his bestselling book *Quality Is Free*, started his career in manufacturing in 1952 at Crosley Corp. in Indiana. After he worked at a series of related manufacturing jobs, Crosby became director of quality for the Pershing missile project at Martin Marietta Corp. He was eminently successful in reducing the manufacturing defects in the production of the missile by embarking on a "zero-defects" program, which later became a government policy. Crosby became famous in government circles because of his success with zero defects, but others who attempted to install the program were less successful, in part says Crosby, because of the lack of management commitment.

Crosby moved to ITT, where he became the corporate vice president of quality and where he started the Quality College to impart the concepts of quality to ITT employees. In 1979, he retired to Winter Park, Florida, where he established the "Quality College" under his new firm, Philip Crosby Associates.

Like W. Edwards Deming, Crosby's approach to quality is also summarized in fourteen steps.

What is the most basic way to determine your quality requirements?

Again, Phil Crosby and many others advise: "Ask the customer or the person who receives or depends upon your output what their requirements are, then ask if you are meeting them." By following that very simple process, the personnel department in what was then a Delco-Remy plant of GM became the quality leader in the plant and spark plug for a productivity advance. Why? Because employees could focus more on their tasks rather than worry about whether their health benefits or vacation time were being handled correctly and on time.

HOW DO YOU ACHIEVE, MANAGE, OR IMPROVE QUALITY?

Dr W. Edwards Deming, one of the early leaders of the modern quality movement, gives this timeless and useful advice, in the March 1988 article in *The Journal for Quality and Participation*:

» *Improving quality:* "Quality is improved in three ways:
  1 through innovation in design of a product or service;
  2 through innovation in processes; and
  3 through improvement of existing processes.

  Hard work will not ensure quality. Best efforts will not ensure quality, and neither will gadgets, computers, or investment in machinery."

» *Managing quality:* "Managing quality begins with honoring five principles.
  1 [Understand variation in systems] The central problem in lack of quality is the failure of management to understand variation. (Everything varies. Statistics help us to predict how much it is going to vary.)
  2 It is management's responsibility to know whether the problems are in the system or in the behavior of the people.
  3 Teamwork should be based on knowledge, design, redesign, and redesign. Constant improvement is management's responsibility. Most causes of low quality and productivity belong to the system.
  4 Train people until they are in statistical control (until they are achieving as much as they can within the limits of the system you are using).
  5 It is management's responsibility to give detailed specifications."

  Deming also developed 14 points to guide managers in their thinking about how to manage quality.

  1 "Create constancy of purpose toward improvement of product and service with a plan to become competitive – to stay in business and to provide jobs.
  2 Adopt a new philosophy. We are in a new economic age. We can no longer live with commonly accepted levels of delays, mistakes, defective materials, and defective workmanship.

3 Cease dependence on mass inspection. Require instead, statistical evidence that quality is built – in to eliminate need for inspection on a mass basis.

4 End the practice of awarding business on the basis of price tag alone. Instead, depend on meaningful measures of quality along with price.

5 Improve constantly and forever the system of production and service. It is management's job to work continually on the system.

6 Institute a vigorous program of education and retraining.

7 Adopt and institute leadership. The responsibility of supervision must be changed from sheer numbers to quality. Improvement of quality will automatically improve productivity.

8 Drive out fear so that everyone may work effectively for the company.

9 Break down barriers between departments. People in research, design, sales, and production must work as a team to foresee problems of production that may be encountered with various materials and specifications.

10 Eliminate numerical goals, posters, and slogans for the workforce that ask for new levels of productivity without providing new methods.

11 Eliminate work standards that prescribe numerical quotas.

12 Remove barriers that stand between the hourly worker and his right to pride of workmanship.

13 Encourage education and self–improvement for everyone.

14 Create a structure in top management that will push every day on the above thirteen points.''

These 14 points may well seem to be too basic to some readers but we have found very few firms or organizations that have applied them consistently over time.

WHAT IS QUALITY DOCUMENTATION AND HOW DOES IT FIT INTO THE LARGER PICTURE?

Documentation of work processes and tracking continuous improvement are key factors to ISO 9000. Basically, companies and institutions are charged with organizing teams from all key departments except those involved in financial services. Employees are asked to document how they conduct their job. Information is shared throughout the specific department and the ideal is that best practices and uniform procedures emerge from this information-sharing process.

WHAT IS ISO 9001? IS IT DIFFERENT FROM ISO 9000?

ISO 9000:2000 incorporates the following:

» ISO 9001 sets out the requirements for an organization whose business processes range all the way from design and development, to production, installation, and servicing.
» ISO 9002 is the appropriate standard for an organization that does not carry out design and development, since it does not include the design control requirements of ISO 9001 – otherwise, its requirements are identical.
» ISO 9003 is the appropriate standard for an organization whose business processes do not include design control, process control, purchasing, or servicing, and which basically uses inspection and testing to ensure that final products and services meet specified requirements.

Have People Always Been Interested in Quality and in Measuring it?

Where and when do we first find a record of people sufficiently concerned with quality and quality management? No one knows. Why? Because people have been concerned with quality goods and services from the moment one person offered something of value to "purchase" a good or service from someone else.

QUALITY SINCE THE BEGINNING OF CIVILIZATION

But we do know that quality and quality management have been important since the dawn of civilization. Ever since the first "purchase" was made for:

» a jar of wine, beer, or oil;
» a sack of grain;
» a weapon;
» some fabric or article of clothing;
» some type of tool; or
» a service to be provided;
» some quantity of land, etc.;

the following questions were commonly asked.

1 How much is being offered?
2 Is it safe to eat, or use?
3 How long will it work?
4 Is this just acceptable, average, or the finest?
5 Is this the newest available?
6 How soon can I have it?
7 Can it be delivered?
8 Can it be modified for my use alone?

EARLY MEASURES OF QUALITY AND QUALITY MANAGEMENT

» By 3000 BC, Sumerians are noting, on clay tablets, how much of something was being traded by repeating symbols, each standing for a "measure" of the good.

» At about 2900 BC, the Pharaoh Khufu decreed that a standard unit of length would be the distance from the tip of his hand to his elbow – the Royal Egyptian Cubit.
» In England, during the reign of Edgar the Peaceful, from 959 AD to 975 AD, it was decreed that all measures must agree with the standards kept in Winchester and London. From that time onwards the bushel and its parts (peck, gallon, etc.) became known as "Winchester measure" and were used for the measurement of all grains and agricultural produce.

In other words, since the publication of the Code of Hammurabi, there has been a *cost* for poor quality: if you sell bad beer or grain or do not fully provide the contracted service, you are in trouble with both the government and consumers.

THE DRIVERS OF CHANGE IN QUALITY EXPECTATIONS

As soon as there was more than one local provider for a service or good, "competition" also began to drive the evolution of quality and quality management. Other factors that drive quality, quality management, and quality improvement in the "modern" era are:

» the ability to mass produce goods and services;
» war;
» improvements in transportation;
» mass communication; and
» the growth of democracy.

As war increased in scope and intensity, the need for large quantities of dependable weapons, as well as support material, transport, and training increased. Improvements in speed, accuracy, and cost of information gave consumers, suppliers, competitors, and regulators the ability to demand improvements from local producers and providers of goods and services.

The growth of democracy as a form of government increased pressure on government to be one of the chief players in assuring safety and accuracy in quality. The growth in the scope and intensity of war meant that the government demanded or required swift improvements in transport, communication, quantity, and quality.

While none of these factors affecting judgment of quality went away, they changed the quality formula considerably. The cost of many types of goods and services dropped dramatically. By 1900, distributors of farm goods alone could see vast new markets opening simply because food could be moved hundreds of miles before it spoiled. Mass production had significantly narrowed the gap between what had been the lowest acceptable quality available and the finest.

This rapid pace of industrialization, as well as increased competition between European and North American producers worldwide, led to the first stirrings of what many would call the first phase of the modern quality movement.

PRE-MODERN QUALITY MANAGEMENT: SCIENTIFIC MANAGEMENT AND FREDERICK TAYLOR

During this period, Frederick W. Taylor was working on how to better organize the entire structure of people, machines, and work processes. When he published his first book in 1911, he called his system "Scientific Management." Working during the same period, Frank and Lillian Gilbreth focused on how specific tasks were done, looking for the best way to complete a task, in the least time, with the least amount of effort.

Mass production of acceptable quality, at reasonable prices, drove interest in fineness of materials, fit and finish, and custom goods into the background. When Henry Ford could deliver an affordable and dependable automobile or truck to any working person who wanted one, who needed fine, handcrafted, custom (or very advanced) designed vehicles? The by-word might have been "let the rich pay for that, I'll wait until the Ford working man's version comes out."

WAR AND QUALITY

The need for rapid advances in preciseness and dependable quantities of war material during the First World War carried knowledge of this first phase of the modern quality movement to nearly every industrial enterprise in the world.

The outbreak of the Second World War would drive the first mass introduction of statistical quality control methods into industry via the requirements of the military in North America.

In talking with people who had worked at Cincinnati Milling Machine (later Cincinnati Milacron and now separate companies Milacron and Cincinnati Machine) during the Second World War and during the war, soon after, in Korea, one of the authors was told, "There were check sheets and control charts all over the place during World War Two and during Korea and sometimes we even had to include them with the shipped product." When asked why the same company considered SPC and quality circles new in the late 1970s, the reply was, "As soon as the requirement was dropped by the military, we stopped using it. Besides, only a few people in the plant ever really knew what they were for and how to use them. This time around, machinists are actually being trained to understand and apply SPC to their work – and not being simply instructed to fill out the charts and let quality control worry about what it means."

After the war, the focus on quality quickly died out. Why had phase 1 of modern quality nearly stopped dead in its tracks? A chief quality driver – competition – had been nearly completely leveled during the war and the US had no significant industrial competitors for nearly a decade. Industry in the UK had not been leveled but it had effectively worn out. The major industrial plants in the rest of Europe had been wiped out. The story was the same in Japan and China.

DEMING, JAPAN, AND THE CALIFORNIAN CONNECTION

Then, W. Edwards Deming, who had published a book on Walter A. Shewhart's methods of quality control in 1944, was asked by General McArthur (then responsible for Japan's recovery) in 1947 to come and help with the Japanese census. Members of the Japanese Union of

Scientists and Engineers (JUSE), who learned of Deming's expertise in quality control, invited him to come and give some talks in 1950. Soon after, Joseph Juran and then Armand V. Feigenbaum were also invited to come to Japan to talk about quality management. Not long after that (1954), Dr Genichi Taguchi (who would lead the quality revolution at Toyota) met Shewhart at a meeting of the Indian Statistical Institute. No one knew it at the time, but the groundwork for the second phase of the modern quality movement had been laid by four Americans who had not yet found as large and accepting an audience in the US as they did in Japan.

The results of the Japanese quality movement began attracting Californian buyers of consumer electronics, cameras, and automobiles during the early and mid-1960s. In less than 10 years, by using Deming's and the other quality experts' methods, they were able to make a credible "Henry Ford" offer to Californian consumers. By the late 1960s and early 1970s, these same producers had begun a new phase. They used consistent high quality at a low to medium-range price (due to their quality-fueled cost savings, a favorable exchange rate, and still lower labor costs) to begin offering top-end quality, superior fit and finish, fine materials, all sorts of "extras," or new features.

A new driver of quality also surfaced at this time – the demonstration effect, for want of a better term. Buyers of a "high quality at reasonable price" product in one sector, consumer electronics for example, began to "assume" that they could or should expect the same in all consumer products. During the late 1970s and 1980s, North American consumer expectations (now joined by European consumers) of good quality at reasonable price outpaced the ability of producers to respond quickly. Xerox, which had "invented" its field, found that Japanese competitors were retailing a comparable product at a cost equal or less than it cost Xerox to build their own product. They decided to "get quality" in a hurry.

THE CATCH-UP PHASE OF QUALITY

During the mid-1980s and early 1990s, fueled by Japanese manu-facturing's rapid advances and well-publicized catch-up campaigns by American companies, the demonstration effect took on a life of its own.

Both retail and business consumers began to assume that everything "should" be available at the highest quality and at a reasonable cost.

Helping this pre-launching of a third phase of quality were writers, speakers, and researchers from across the globe, telling the world that high quality at reasonable cost was not an accident or a national characteristic – anyone could do it with sufficient effort and commitment. Then, during the late 1980s, first the US, then Europe and other nations, launched national quality award processes to support "national" improvements in quality.

PHASE THREE: ISO 9000 AND THE "PERMANENT" QUALITY REVOLUTION

In one sense, the third phase of quality becomes official when the ISO 9000 standard for quality management "takes off." Although ISO 9000 was launched in 1987, it was during the mid-1990s that it reached a take-off stage and there was rapid adoption of it across the board in several influential, or supply-chain-leading industries. By the end of the 1990s, quality management, products, and services are no longer an extra or an add-on; it's a "requirement" for being in business beyond the "mom and pop" level.

ISO 9000 has its earliest origins in the emergence of quality system registration or testing, which the United States military started promoting during the Second World War and then transferred to NATO allies. Influenced by the strategic demand for quality military equipment produced in a timely fashion, the Allies developed the so-called AQAPs (Allied Quality Assurance Publications). The British and Dutch eventually developed national industrial standards for quality systems based on the AQAPs, out of which the British Standards Institution (BSI) developed its own quality program called BS 5750.

In 1980, ISO formed Technical Committee (TC) 176 to develop international standards for quality management and quality assurance. Using BS 5750 as a base, TC 176 eventually designed and had ISO publish the first ISO 9000 series in 1987.

Although the ISO 9000 standards series has been criticized through the years as providing more of an emphasis on consistency – particularly in manufacturing – than on quality, it has managed to survive through several revisions and continued development of industry-specific hybrids.

The original ISO 9000:1987 standard series included the following:

» ISO 9000: a description of the standard series;
» ISO 9001: for "complete" companies that research, design, build, ship, install, and service products;
» ISO 9002: for companies that produce and install products;
» ISO 9003: for warehousing and distribution companies;
» ISO 9004: serves mainly as a guidance document.

The first major revision of ISO 9000 took place in 1994, which enlarged the standard's focus from manufacturing only, to process materials, services, and software. An emphasis on generic product categories was added, instead of on manufactured goods and hardware. The revisions also offered more guidelines to registrars conducting the audits that lead to ISO 9000 registration (certification in Europe), and introduced the idea of quality plans to be used in the design phase of a project, and to be required for each product produced or each service offered. Other changes involved expansion of elements covered in the original standards series and a closing of auditing loopholes so that companies had to demonstrate more fully reasons for excluding aspects of the ISO 9000 process.

The standards series was most recently revised in 2000 to reflect continual criticism that it alone could not provide the quality benefits that its boosters claimed. Companies and industries worldwide also complained that there wasn't enough focus on elements of continuous improvement and customer satisfaction from what is known as total quality management (TQM) or TQM's latest variant, "Six Sigma."

The new ISO 9000 standards series – called ISO 9000:2000 – became official on December 14, 2000. Any company which now has an ISO 9000 certificate has three years to comply with the new requirements, many of which are focused on the quality process, including customer satisfaction, communication, and continuous improvement.

The new series has been streamlined and includes the following:

» DIS 9000: 2000, Quality Management Systems – Fundaments and vocabulary;
» DIS 9000: 2000, Quality Management Systems – Requirements; and
» DIS 9000: 2000, Quality Management Systems – Guidelines for Performance Management.

The new series presupposes that companies have clearly delineated business goals and have some sense of tracking the changes that will lead to continuous improvement. To attain this goal, experts advise companies and their registrars to build a relationship that will promote a quality progress. Few, if any, companies will have to re-earn a certificate from scratch. Experts say that those companies that do not have mature quality systems in place and have not focused on building continuous improvement into their daily business will have the most problem with the new standard. They can start remedying the situation right now by examining how they have implemented ISO 9000.

THE ISO 9000 HYBRIDS

Within seven years of its original publication date, specific industries started developing their own variations of ISO 9000. In 1994, the Big Three automakers – General Motors, Ford Motor Co., and the then Chrysler Corp. – announced development of QS-9000. This standard utilizes the ISO 9000 quality base while introducing industry-specific guidelines drawn from former auto industry programs. Both GM and Chrysler – now DaimlerChrysler – mandated QS-9000 for all suppliers internationally, while only Ford has insisted on compliance.

In 1996, ISO published a variant of ISO 9000 for environmental management called ISO 14000. That same year they published special requirements for medical devices – ISO 13485 – that include an ISO 9000 quality base.

In the late 1990s, other industries also developed their own ISO 9000 variants. AS 9000 for aerospace was published under the auspices of the American Aerospace Quality Group (AAQG) in October 1996 through the Society of Automotive Engineers (SAE), which eventually became a sponsor. A slightly revised version was released in 1997 and an international variant – SAE-AS 91000 – was formally published in

November 1999 by SAE and is now mandatory for all Boeing suppliers. The same standard is published in Europe as prEN9100.[1]

Then in 2000, the QuEST Forum – a group of major telecommunication companies – published TL 9000. For the most part TL 9000 is still a voluntary standard. It was being updated in 2001.[2]

QUALITY TIMELINE

Each society has its own history of establishing measures and means to assure quality of goods and services. The very early examples are just that: a few early examples of how and when measures were established. The advance in quality and quality management is often noted simply by the publication date of a book significant to the movement.

The beginning of quality measurement begins with establishing measures:

» **3000 BC**: The Sumerians were drawing images of tokens on clay tablets. At this point, different types of goods were represented by different symbols, and multiple quantities represented by repetition.
» **2900 BC**: The Pharaoh Khufu was the first to decree that a standard unit of length should be fixed. The standard chosen was made of black granite and was called the Royal Egyptian Cubit. History records its length as that of the Pharaoh's forearm and hand.
» **959 AD to 975 AD**: During the reign of Edgar the Peaceful in England, it was decreed that all measures must agree with the standards kept in Winchester and London.
» **1791**: "Jefferson Report." Thomas Jefferson described England's weights and measures standards to Congress "on the supposition that the present measures are to be retained."
» **1821**: "Adams Report." John Quincy Adams recommended to Congress that they act to bring about uniformity in weights and measures, and described France's young metric system as a praiseworthy attempt at uniformity.

» **1884**: The IPA (International Participation Association (UK)) in its first guise was formed as The Labour Association for Promoting Cooperative Production Amongst the Workforce.

The modern quality movement

» **1903**: *Shop Management*, Frank and Lillian Gilbreth.
» **1911**: *The Principles of Scientific Management*, Frederick W. Taylor.
» **1912**: The Society for the Advancement of Management SAM® was founded as the Taylor Society by the colleagues and disciples of Frederick Taylor, the "Father of Scientific Management."
» **1916**: *Fatigue Study*, Frank and Lillian Gilbreth.
» **1917**: World War I works councils' shop committees represent American industry's first formal experience with joint worker–management problem-solving teams. Based on President Wilson's reading and understanding of a "white paper" produced in Great Britain by the Labour Association for Promoting Cooperative Production Amongst the Workforce in 1913–14.
» **1926**: *Application of Statistics in Maintaining Quality of a Manufactured Product, and Quality Control Charts*, Shewhart, W.A.
» **1931**: *Economic Control of Quality of Manufactured Product*, Shewhart, W.A.
» **1942**: USA War Production Board created campaign to encourage employers and unions to start voluntary labor–management committees in their plants.
» **1944**: *Some Principles of the Shewhart Methods of Quality Control*, Deming, W. Edwards.
» **1946 (Feb)**: 17 local quality control societies formed the American Society for Quality Control. (**May**): The Japanese Union of Scientists and Engineering (JUSE) established.
» **1948**: The Institute of Industrial Engineers (IIE) established. "An approach to the study of some of the behavior patterns of industrial organization," Thesis for management M.S., by Armand Vallin Feigenbaum.

» **1950**: JUSE invited Deming to come to Japan and deliver a series of lectures on quality (some JUSE members had met Deming on his earlier visit to Japan in 1947 to assist with their census).

» **1950–52**: Use of SPC mandated for use in manufacturing of certain US military supplies.

» **1951**: *Quality Control Handbook*, J.M. Juran. The Deming Prize was created in 1951 by JUSE.

» **1954**: The Union of Japanese Scientists and Engineers invited J.M. Juran to carry out a series of conferences and seminars on statistical process control. Dr Genichi Taguchi was visiting Professor at the Indian Statistical Institute. During this visit, he met the famous statisticians R.A. Fisher and Walter A. Shewhart. Courses in quality control are organized for foremen by JUSE.

» **1955**: JUSE QC Middle Management Course.

» **1956**: JUSE team visits IBM typewriter plant headed by Claire Vough. Note in a letter that they are very impressed by the workshop committees and the training of all employees in work simplification and craftsmanship.

» **1957**: JUSE QC Top Management Course. *Design of Experiments*, Dr Genichi Taguchi

» **1958**: *QC Circle Activities*, Kaoru Ishikawa, Editor.

» **1961**: *Total Quality Control - Engineering and Management*, Feigenbaum, A.V.

» **1966**: Quality Function Deployment (QFD) was introduced in Japan by Yoji Akao.

» **1974**: A team of engineers from Lockheed visits Japan to investigate use of QC Circles. QC Circles begun later that year at Lockheed.

» **1977**: International Association for Quality Circles (later Association for Quality and Participation: 1989) founded.

» **1978**: First conference in US on Quality Circle activities meets in San Francisco, California.

» **1979**: *Productivity: A Practical Program for Improving Efficiency*, Clair Vough, Bernard Asbell. *Management For Quality Improvement: The 7 New QC Tools*, Shigeru Mizuno. *Quality Is Free*, Crosby, Philip B.

» **1980–81**: Mass training in quality improvement as part of a joint labor–management agreement begins at General Motors.
» **1982**: *Out of the Crisis*, Deming, W. Edwards. *Guide to Quality Control*, Ishikawa, Kaoru.
» **1984**: IAQC (now AQP) holds first Team Excellence competition and awards process. McDonell Douglas quality circle wins top honors. NBC television airs "If Japan Can, Why Can't We?"
» **1985**: *A Passion for Excellence: The Leadership Difference*, Peters, Tom and Nancy K. Austin.
» **1986**: Masaaki Imai established the Kaizen Institute to help Western companies introduce kaizen concepts, systems, and tools. That same year, he published his book on Japanese management, *Kaizen: The Key to Japan's Competitive Success*.
» **1987**: ISO 9000 is published.
» **1987–88**: Malcolm Baldrige National Quality Award is established. In 1988, Motorola was first winner. In 1988, The European Foundation for Quality Management (EFQM) was founded.
» **1993**: *The New Economics For Industry, Government, Education*, Deming, W. Edwards.
» **1994**: The *Fifth Discipline*, Senge, Peter M. ISO 9000 is revised. Auto industry in US establishes QS 9000, a joint quality standard to replace the standards each had been using.
» **1995**: The W. Edwards Deming Institute is established one year after Dr Deming's death.
» **2000**: ISO 9000 is revised.
» **2001**: The AQP (Association for Quality and Participation) merges with ASQ, the American Society for Quality.

NOTES

1 Source is Eugene Barker, Certified Quality Manager, Boeing Technical Fellow, and The Boeing Commercial Airlines Group.
2 Material is adapted from *ISO 9000 MADE EASY: A Cost-Saving Guide to Documentation and Registration* by Amy Zuckerman, formerly AMACOM Books and now published by A–Z International Associates, Amherst, MA.

Quality Management and the E-Dimension: What's the Connection?

» More information on quality than you can digest, even in several sittings
» End-use customers, retail or B2B (business-to-business) customers can comparison-shop like they never could before
» Virtual quality improvement processes
  » Sun Microsystems
» The e-dimension of ISO 9000

Like everything about the Internet/Web, this enormous electronic transmission pipeline creates opportunities and headaches for managers and their operations.

On the plus side, the ability to transmit data and information instantaneously worldwide and conduct your business in cyberspace means faster and more efficient means of tagging quality efforts throughout a supply chain or supply network. On the negative side, those who don't practice quality control in terms of information flow and accuracy will find themselves quickly up to their ears in alligators.

As one top executive of a major bank and credit card company explained, in the pre-Internet days one error used to affect about 5000 customers. Nowadays, with the Internet, the same mistake can affect 5 million customers and in a matter of minutes, not days or weeks.

Let's look at a number of ways that the e-world is affecting the quality movement and your quality efforts. Then we'll explore how the Internet/Web are affecting ISO 9000 and the standards certification arena.

MORE INFORMATION ON QUALITY THAN YOU CAN DIGEST, EVEN IN SEVERAL SITTINGS

The first obvious impact of the Internet on quality and quality management is the explosion of information available – free and for a fee.

A 10-second search with a meta-search engine (a search engine that simultaneously queries 2–100 search engines) on the Internet enables anyone in any organization to "find" literally thousands of pages and sites filled with the best and worst information about quality and quality management. There are three ways to avoid getting lost in figuring out which information is worthwhile and which is not.

1 Purchase, or check out of the library, one or two of the books we will recommend in the resources section.
2 Visit two or more of the not-for-profit professional organizations, or government agencies, that will be listed in the resources section and search their databases of books, articles, and conference presentations.
3 Visit several of the "grassroots" individual Web pages that we will recommend in the resources section.

For those interested in the statistical side of quality, we have found numerous sites where you can download entirely serviceable and robust statistical software (The National Institute of Science and Technology (www.nist.gov) is just one of those sites). And beyond those sources, for those interested in virtual resources, there are a number of marvelous university and "grassroots" Websites with Java-based statistical tools that can be used online in real time! (We will also list some of the best of these sites in the resources section.)

END-USE CUSTOMERS, RETAIL OR B2B (BUSINESS-TO-BUSINESS) CUSTOMERS CAN COMPARISON-SHOP LIKE THEY NEVER COULD BEFORE

Recently, one of the authors observed a shopper in a local grocery store comparison-shopping on almost every item on his computer-generated shopping list. He was on his Internet-capable cell phone with his wife, who was assisting at home in front of their home computer. When asked why he was on the phone and the Internet at the same time, when he already had a list from the Internet, he replied: "This store has a policy of honoring all company coupons and that they will match the lowest available price in Cincinnati. This way, we can access – and I can print out the coupons or price listing with the mini-printer that connects up with the PDA in my backpack – prices and coupons that change during the day." B2B consumers have the same array of tools available to them.

These customers are not just price shopping; they are quality and price shopping. And the Internet with its host of customer portal sites enables them to drill as far down as they wish to determine what is the best at the best price.

FROM PLANETFEEDBACK.COM
See which companies make the grade, according to your letters!

Grade A
» Lands' End
» Mary Kay, Inc.

» Drugstore.com
» Sephora.com
» Krispy Kreme

"You didn't have the company listed on your site, but I had the ability to send the letter myself. I have already received a reply and the company is going to send me TWO of their latest-model remote fans to replace the shoddy ones I had purchased. I never expected such a generous offer . . . Thanks, PlanetFeedback!"

– Mary M., Houston, Texas

In a long-running children's cartoon, there is a mythical company, Acme, which delivers all sorts of devices to either the roadrunner or coyote character. That mythical Acme will soon become a reality on the Internet. When it arrives, it will offer 24 hours a day and seven days a week to fulfill all of the quality requirements that customers ordinarily require. Their offer will be something like this: "What you want, the way you want it, where and when you want it, at your price!"

Too audacious? In 1990, Professor Hidaki Yoshihara from Kobe University in a *Journal for Quality and Participation* article entitled "Originality in Management" wrote about a custom bicycle system. He said it "is an easy-order system by which a customer goes to a bicycle shop, orders a bicycle that fits his or her body structure and, two weeks later, receives the custom-made product." That was pre-Internet. Here is a year 2001 Internet site's "online" offer:

The BC USA custom bike designer has taken the next evolutionary step. Our menu of over 1000 choices for your custom bike is unmatched anywhere. You get the best selection, most accurate and thorough information, and the best prices as well.

Before we discuss the impact of the Internet on ISO 9000 and quality documentation, there are two additional Internet quality opportunities that will grow in importance over time.

VIRTUAL QUALITY IMPROVEMENT PROCESSES

The Internet, via virtual private networks (VPNs) and company intranets, has enabled pioneering companies to pull together a variety of quality efforts – from problem solving to training. An area related to quality, just-in-time manufacturing and delivery systems, has enabled many firms to improve productivity and quality by cutting time and costs out of their systems. The problem has been resolving problems, in time, when lead times are so short. The Internet now gives companies the ability to conduct extensive, real-time problem solving and prevention work. As the robustness of VPN security improves sufficiently, to satisfy those who are now justifiably cautious about their use, this area will grow in importance to companies and governments. A second area that will benefit from greater use of the Internet for improving and sustaining quality is supply chain management. An area closely related to that, which will also benefit from greater use of the Internet, is the growing number of partnerships or alliances between companies to jointly produce or market products or services. As the security of databases and the exchange of data improve, this area will also grow quickly in importance and use.

QUALITY OF THE INTERNET

Everyone knows that the Internet is delivering much more than was ever expected of it. That's the problem. The Internet and its use have far outstripped anyone's ability to address its "quality" issues. At this time, a film parody entitled "Lost in Cyberspace" would produce as many winces as laughs. Those involved with development of the Internet are using quality methods but the results to date tell us that too few people and resources are currently devoted to the effort.

All of the advances in the quality of other products and services have created an expectation that the Internet must live up to soon. Why? When the public, this time a public in more than 100 nations, really wants a service, *it really wants it*. And if it is being delivered poorly, it will demand that their respective governments do something about it. Differences in how privacy issues are viewed in the US and the EU are an early warning bell on future issues. The stricter EU privacy policies will impact the quality of information available to retailers in the US and Europe.

THE E-DIMENSION OF ISO 9000

Companies and institutions can't get any bang from their technology, practice knowledge management, or even contemplate operating in a networked, Web-based environment – let alone practice business-to-business (B2B) electronic commerce without open communication flow throughout their organizations.

Although ISO 9000 is usually thought of as a quality tool, it can be quite a potent organizing force, as well as human communication model, for a networked company. When organizations pursue ISO 9000 as a process, rather than just hiring out to "pass a test" and earn an ISO 9000 certificate, they will inevitably open improved communication channels throughout their organizations. It's this shift from a hierarchical to an employee-involvement model that sets the stage for the circular sort of communication that networking requires, and sets the stage for electronic commerce and a Web-based organization.

Here's how. Because ISO 9000 encourages employee involvement in both documentation of work procedures and data control, that means it contains a strong communication component. It's this component that smart organizations find helpful in addressing corporate communication issues, which can be problematic for many organizations, especially when they implant advanced technologies that require open information and communication flow.

When companies set up a common language for their work procedures, they are creating the basis for improved communication and information flow between management and employees, offices, departments, suppliers, and customers. This is the structure required to run an effective supply chain on a regional or even global basis.

By involving employees in a team approach to gather, sort, and cull information on work procedures, companies will not only create an easy-to-maintain documentation system required to earn ISO 9000 registration. They will be providing the foundation for employees to practice information management, key to efficient supply chain management, and which serves as a basis for knowledge management and electronic commerce.[1]

BEST PRACTICE CASE STUDY

Sun Microsystems is one of the few backbone-of-the-Internet and networking companies to consistently focus on customer issues as the means to organize their quality improvement processes. The quality initiative, championed by Sun Microsystems CEO Scott McNealy, has helped Sun maintain its status as a global Fortune 500 leader in enterprise network computing. Sun's quality initiative has its roots in a decision made by McNealy in 1993 to formalize the company's quality direction and to promote quality among employees.

Sun began its quality journey by focusing outward – inviting Paul Allaire from Xerox, Fred Smith from Federal Express and Gary Tooker who was then the CEO of Motorola to a meeting between Sun's executives and their executives. Sun heard how they were driving quality throughout their organizations and the consistent message heard was that you really need to get your frontline employees engaged.

SunTeams are voluntary, grassroots employee teams that form to handle process improvement that is focused on driving down dissatisfiers and working on issues that drive up the customer loyalty. SunTeams have been formed across all departments and divisions of Sun and have been key factors in raising customer satisfaction levels. They had approximately 70 voluntary teams worldwide after about six months.

CEO Scott McNealy does a monthly interview on W-SUN that is broadcast to all Sun employees. He interviews people from different parts of the company and periodically interviews team leaders, sponsors, and members involved in this process improvement effort. These interviews not only build awareness of the quality process, it gives recognition to the efforts of individual teams and team sponsors. Each year Sun recognizes the "best of the best" at a company-wide celebration profiling the highest-performing SunTeams.

The basic quality driver for Sun Microsystems is to drive customer loyalty satisfiers up and dissatisfiers down: Using an independent organization, thousands of Sun Microsystems customers are interviewed on a regular basis throughout the year. They track the resulting customer loyalty index to see how satisfied customers are. They used those surveys to identify the top 50 customer dissatisfiers and then measure their improvement efforts on driving down those dissatisfiers. Their quality vision was very simple – drive up the customer loyalty index and drive down the dissatisfiers.

Sun worked with Xerox to license and "Sun-ize" Xerox's problem-solving methodology. Teams across the company, no matter where they are, in which division or in which country, are all using similar problem-solving and process-improvement methodology. The benefit is that they can have virtual teams all over the world. The teams are all speaking the same language and they're attacking the problems in process improvement using the same methodology.

VIRTUAL TEAMS

Virtual teams are quality improvement teams made up of members who may share an interest in, or have a key part in, the process under study for improvement but are not located at the same facility or even work in the same state or country. While virtual teams could and did exist prior to the build-out of the World Wide Web (WWW) in 1994–95, they were much more expensive and took longer to address problems since members had to be gathered from around the country or the world and scheduled to meet at a common location. One of the early WWW virtual Sun teams, which had members from seven different countries where Sun had facilities, did meet in one location for their first meeting but conducted further meetings and team business with the Internet acting as their "common location." As experience with teamwork in general grew, use of virtual teams also grew to address a wide variety of issues that crossed departmental as well as geographical boundaries.

Using the company's intranet to assure the quality of their team-based process improvement program

Sun Microsystems uses its internal network, its intranet, as an elementary quality tool to assure that its teams are following a consistent process and have the resources necessary for the selected task. The use of the intranet ensures that everybody – the team, Sun Corporate Quality, the teams' immediate quality managers, and Sun's training program – are on the same page and aware of what's going on with the team.

To begin the process, after forming, the Sun team would go online at the Corporate Quality division's Website and fill out what was called a SunTeam's planner. At that time, it was a one-pager that asked for key information that all teams should be thinking about before they have formed as a team anyway.

» Who is their internal, or external, customer?
» What are their goals?
» Who is on the team?
» Who is their sponsor, etc.?

The completed form was sent automatically to corporate quality for tracking purposes. The information also went directly to their quality office within the team's own division. That quality office was made up of key quality managers. These people contacted the team leaders who submitted the information. They identified if the team needed any help in working through their process and determined what they could do to help to make the team be more successful.

The information from the online form also went to Sun University. Someone from the Sun education arm then called the team leader to verify that they'd had the problem-solving and process-improvement training. Sun University also examined what their other needs were and directed them toward the type of training their team could get.

TIMELINE FOR TEAM FORMATION AND IMPROVEMENT PROCESS: VARIABLE

Key insights

» A company intranet can serve effectively as a means to assure the integrity of the organization's quality management process.
» A common basic training process and common set of process-improvement tools establishes a common "organizational language"[2] which in turn facilitates the formation of "virtual" teams. This common organizational quality management language makes adoption of standards such as ISO 9000 or TL 9000 a much easier task as well.[3]

NOTES

1 Source is "ISO 9000: Leverage ISO 9000 for Added Value and Bottom-Line Benefits" by Amy Zuckerman, *Fortune* magazine, May 11, 1998.

2 While there has not been, to our knowledge, a worldwide study of how many companies use a common set of training materials or approaches, a review of the literature indicates that as many companies use a variety of training materials as use a set common to all divisions of a company. In the absence of a common training program throughout an organization, the ISO 9000 framework establishes a common organizational quality management language that facilitates quality management and improvement processes in the same way a common training program would.

3 Material drawn from an interview in 1999 with Linda Welsh, then corporate SunTeams' development manager for Sun Microsystems, Inc.

What are the Implications of Globalization on Quality?

- » ISO 9000 puts the global stamp on quality management
- » Global quality comes to Main Street
- » Quality and affordable cost are now seen as, or expected to be, universal customer requirements
- » Issues of confusion and tension: which standard do I sign up for?
    - » Stand pat with QS-9000–1998 or prepare and go for ISO/TS 16949?
    - » AEROSPACE: AS 9000 and/or SAE AS 9100?
    - » Medical devices: which way to turn?
    - » Cyclone Hardware P&N Tools

Any doubts about the "global-ness" of quality management should have been erased when "We're Proud to be ISO 9002 Certified" banners and ads began appearing on the manufacturing rows in Japan, the UK, Germany, France, Italy, the US, Mexico, Brazil, and Canada.

ISO 9000 PUTS THE GLOBAL STAMP ON QUALITY MANAGEMENT

ISO 9000 has always been an international standard designed, in part, to promote global trade. So there's a bit of irony in the fact that ISO has been playing catch-up with various industries like auto and medical devices and has devised global standards for their industry-specific variants of ISO 9000 – itself a global standard.

GLOBAL QUALITY COMES TO MAIN STREET

The impact of the "global" economy arrived at the front door of US, UK, French, Italian, and German consumers and businesses when products and services that were a part of daily life or somehow connected with national identity "had" to compete with "global" companies. Although many did not realize it at first, global quality management had also arrived, for quality management was a key ingredient that "backed up" Japan's automakers' low-price entry into the North American market. In North America "all of a sudden," Toyota, Nissan (then Datsun) and Honda dealers joined VW and the old Big Three of GM, Ford, and Chrysler in their local version of the *Auto Mall*. For European consumers and businesses quite used to Europe-wide competition, that same awareness of globalization might not have struck home until they realized that American products were as plentiful in local grocery shops as American films, television programs, and music were for the public's eyes and ears.

The 1990s brought globalization to *Main Street* and at a pace that few would have reckoned possible. And what role did quality and quality management have on or in this globalization of the economy? Listen to what the researchers and experts have said about quality and globalization.

In a 1991 report for the Sakura Research Institute, on Japanese subsidiaries in the Asia–Pacific Region, Dennis Tachiki reported that by 1988, the Asia–Pacific area, North America, and Western Europe accounted for 90 percent of the (then 4000) Japanese subsidiaries overseas. What was the importance of quality and quality management to those overseas subsidiaries? Tachiki notes, "we found overseas Japanese subsidiaries are integrating quality control activities into their organization practices first into: strategic planning; measurement systems; and performance evaluations. Quality control circles are being introduced later on."

Mr Nagao Yoshida, Secretary-General of the Asian Productivity Organization, noted at a special presentation at the International Convention of Quality Control Circles (ICQCC91) that "the 1990s will be a pivotal decade for the region" and that "there is a dire need to shift business orientation from a production-intensity phase to a management-intensity phase, with total quality management as one of the pillars in our drive for productivity improvement."

In a 1996 article, Dr Armand V. Feigenbaum said, "companies must now be able to design, build, and sell domestic product lines ... for supremacy in the international marketplace – even though, at present, there may not be much import competition or interest in exporting in your particular product or service."

Echoing, in a sense, decisions already made by thousands of Japanese companies, Feigenbaum noted that "the wide diversity of cultural and product requirements makes quality the only realistic economy of scale for international companies." And he noted, in the same article, that, "Buying in terms of [quality] value has become a highly developed new skill, for both consumers and companies." Peter Totterdill of the Center for Work & Technology at The Nottingham Trent University notes in "Competitive Advantage in the 1990s and Beyond": "Competitiveness must be achieved by means of a strong commitment to innovation, quality, customization, responsiveness to the market and versatility, rather than by price alone."

In short, quality improvement and quality management have been consciously used to advance competitive advantage for individual companies, as well as being a vital part of a national strategy.

QUALITY AND AFFORDABLE COST ARE NOW SEEN AS OR EXPECTED TO BE UNIVERSAL CUSTOMER REQUIREMENTS

Feigenbaum noted that the new marketplace was one in which "No one anywhere in the world wants second-class products nor second-class lives indefinitely anymore." "During the 1990s," Feigenbaum said, "buyers have become convinced through widespread advertising and media attention that any company can provide essentially perfect quality – if it is well enough managed to do so. Our survey data for last year shows that nine out of 10 buyers now make quality their primary purchasing standard but they now express this as affordable quality – quality and price, but also time saving and service – not simply as a trade-off between quality and price."

The case for quality and quality management cascaded into the world marketplace first to satisfy customers, then to companies that supplied consumer companies with their input, then to all suppliers.

When consumers all over the world "discovered" that they should be able to get quality and at an "affordable" price, they had a simple message to business: "We want it and we want it now!"

» The response of companies was, and still is, to "get" quality to satisfy retail consumers.

When companies discovered that they had to have quality, they then looked for ways to assure themselves of quality supplies.

» The response of national business groups to "their need" for quality supplies was to establish first national and then international standards for quality management.

ISSUES OF CONFUSION AND TENSION: WHICH STANDARD DO I SIGN UP FOR?

Given the relatively short time frame for all these changes, it is no surprise that the switch from quantity at low price to quality at affordable price has been accompanied by a good bit of confusion and no small amount of tension. This "you don't have any other choice" atmosphere around quality and quality management comes sharply into focus in the issues surrounding ISO 9000.

Whether to continue pursuing ISO 9000 or move on to an industry-specific hybrid like auto's QS-9000 or telecommunication's TL 9000 has been confusing the world since the release of QS-9000 in 1994 and TL 9000 in 2000. The Big Three automakers addressed that issue for their supply base when they decreed that anyone earning registration to QS-9000 would automatically earn an ISO 9000 certificate. Some suppliers actually decided to pursue both separately for internal or marketing reasons.

To complicate the matter further, anyone in these industries has to decide whether to pursue transition to ISO 9000:2000 – the latest revision of ISO 9000, to stick with the industry-specific variant, or move to a global standard for their industry that's based on ISO 9000.

For organizations caught in this quandary, experts offer the same practical advice given when ISO 9000 was first introduced: If your customers are requiring ISO 9000 or an ISO 9000 industry-specific or equivalent registration as a contract or bidding condition, you will have to implement a quality system and be registered.

Some companies, such as 3M, may not require that your firm be registered to both ISO 9000 and ISO 14000 (environmental quality system), but will give the nod to bidders who are registered, all other items being equal. The result is the same, you should get registered. But "get registered to what standard?" and "does this mean multiple registrations and audits for us?" are questions still left out there for some. For those answers, we went to the experts and people in the field.

AUTOMAKERS

Stand pat with QS-9000–1998 or prepare and go for ISO/TS 16949? In 2000, the world was introduced to ISO/TS 16949, the global equivalent to QS-9000. Although the Big Three automakers had a role in the standard's development, as of 2001 they were not willing to recommend suppliers drop QS-9000 in favor of the international variant.

Generally, automotive experts warn suppliers to be careful to meet customer demand. Ford and GM, for example, have sent memos to their suppliers stating they will recognize ISO/TS 16949 as an equivalent to QS-9000 on a trial basis. They made it clear that registration to the global variant was optional. But some companies like Fiat have gone one step further and said that all their suppliers will now be ISO/TS 16949 compliant. French and German automakers are also expected to endorse the global version.

Some experts in the registration industry believe that anyone who wants to be a worldwide supplier will have to meet ISO/TS 16949 and not just QS-9000. ISO/TS 16949 is being upgraded and will be mirror ISO 9000:2000 in the near future. The chief benefit and reason to move to ISO/TS 16949 is straightforward – ISO/TS 16949 eliminates multiple audits.[1]

AEROSPACE

AS 9000 and/or SAE AS 9100? In aerospace, as in the automotive industry, industry leaders work with their suppliers and with other industry leaders to advance quality for the entire industry. AS 9100 was developed by the ISO Aerospace Technical Committee 20, Working Group 11, in association with international groups representing interested parties in Europe, Brazil, China, Japan, and Mexico. It harmonizes aerospace requirements and is being adopted globally.

Boeing has posted the following message to suppliers on its Website: "Boeing will focus on transitioning its supplier base to AS 9100:1999 as the first step in achieving standardization across the Boeing Enterprise. When AS 9100–2001 is released, it will be evaluated for incorporation and plans will be developed as appropriate. However, to simplify the initial transition of Boeing's supplier base to the new BQMS standard, the expectation is for Boeing suppliers to transition to AS 9100:1999. Transition to AS 9100:2001 will be addressed after Boeing's supplier base has been standardized on AS 9100:1999." Boeing suppliers have two years to implement the standard.

Aerospace suppliers recommend those pursuing any variant of AS 9000 keep their quality process focused on real manufacturing processes and document them to meet their customer's requirements and audit team. Think of ISO 9000:2000 as basic quality criteria that serve as a jumping-off spot for industry-specific requirements. ISO 9000:2000 becomes the foundation and the other standards extensions of it.

It's also advised to seriously consider implementing a simple and enforceable weekly audit – an ISO 9000 dashboard of critical indicators – that links the ISO 9000 elements which are critical to a basic ISO system by putting them in a simple spreadsheet for weekly management team audits. If you audit these critical elements each week, then you do not have to do a hurry-up audit right before the registrar, supplier auditor, or your corporate auditor shows up. Always remember that the ISO 9000 family serves you best when you don't focus on passing a test, but on how to use the process to improve your operation.[2]

MEDICAL DEVICES: WHICH WAY TO TURN?

The medical device industry faces a great deal of regulation from individual countries and regions. Manufacturers concerned with meeting those regulations need to bear in mind that ISO 9000:2000 won't help them meet specific government regulations.

ISO 13485 appears to be the best bet for many companies. It incorporates elements of ISO 9000 and ISO 46000, which is the harmonized European standard for medical devices, and puts them into the principles of an international standard. At this time, ISO 13485 is being revised to adapt to the new ISO 9000:2000 requirements, while still retaining the basic requirements of the 1994 version of ISO 9000. The new ISO 13485 is still in draft document form. A new standard is expected sometime in 2002.

When trying to decide what to do, companies should bear in mind that ISO 9000:2000 is not a prerequisite for either the European Directive or FDA. It may provide commercial benefits, but not regulatory ones. For companies that can wait, it's suggested you pursue the new version of ISO 13485, which requires documentation and procedures that fit in line with regulatory expectations of agencies such as the FDA.

But if you need to earn ISO 9000 for a specific customer, beware that ISO 13485 drops the particularly continuous improvement and customer satisfaction elements that aren't pertinent in a regulatory environment. You may find you have to earn registration to both standards.[3]

BEST PRACTICE

Cyclone Hardware P&N Tools

Cyclone Hardware P&N Tools manufactures products for the building and engineering industries. Over the years, imports have been reducing P&N Tools' marketshare, while at the same time the recession has reduced the overall market demand. This has led to casual employee lay-offs, four-day working weeks, and minimal capital expenditure on new technology. The current workforce is approximately 160 and most employees work a day/afternoon shift operation.

The work redesign process used at Cyclone Hardware P&N Tools' plant in central Victoria, Australia, was based on the work of Australians Drs Fred and Merrelyn Emery.

Initially a design team was selected to review the way work was organized from a macro perspective. A new structure was developed requiring only three levels: because when you have those doing the work taking responsibility for controlling and coordinating it, there is less need for direct supervision. Once this structure was developed it was then a matter of taking each of the teams through a participative design workshop. This micro analysis either supported or enhanced the initial macro structure.

In all cases, the teams stayed with the three-level structure and had no role for a first-line supervisor, or lead person. A role of coordinator or team spokesperson was to be rotated within each team. After the teams developed their new way of working, they then had to determine how their new design would work.

One of the self-managing teams at P&N Tools set itself the following goals, which in turn were negotiated with management.

1 Build up stock levels before the Christmas shutdown . . .
2 Reduce machine setup times by 50 percent . . .
3 Reduce scrap by from 1.5 percent to 0.5 percent . . .
4 Reduce absenteeism by 50 percent . . .
5 No more than two lost time injuries per annum.

As this team worked on providing adequate stock cover, they realized they had 1600 hours of work ahead of them, but only a 1200-hour window within which to complete it. The team overcame this problem by producing a roster system that made better use of the machines during smoke breaks and lunch, and calling on other internal resources when available.

Once multi-skilling training had taken place, team members began requesting TQM/JIT tools and techniques to reduce the cost of quality and increase output. This has enabled maintenance personnel to concentrate on issues such as critical breakdowns and preventative maintenance.

[At the time of writing, Cyclone Hardware P&N Tools' overall performance and product demand has improved to such an extent that a third production shift has been introduced.][4]

THE INTERNATIONAL MISSION OF TQC – APPLYING TQC TO SAFETY IN NUCLEAR POWER (1991)

Shiochiro Kobayashi – Chairman of the Board, The Kansai Electric Power Company, Ltd

"Ten years have passed since we introduced TQC to our company. In retrospect of the path we have followed, we now fully realize how important the international mission of total quality control is.

"When, in 1983, I met the chairman of the Florida Power & Light Company of the United States, who had come to

Japan to attend the US–Japan Summit Meeting on Electric Power, and told him that we had come to grips with TQC, he became deeply interested in it and later introduced it to his company too.

"While we concluded an 'Agreement for Exchanging Information on Quality Control' with his firm for the purpose of mutually enlightening each other, we gave support to it by sending to Florida some of our staff who were thoroughly vested in TQC. These efforts eventually bore fruit; last year the Florida Power & Light Company was awarded the Deming Application Prize, marking the first time a company outside Japan ever earned this award.

"The profound significance that we place on the fact that the Florida Power & Light Company received the prize is that, for example, if an accident occurs in relation to nuclear power today, the problem may have its effects beyond the nation in which it happens. As shown by the Chernobyl meltdown, such a problem can have far-reaching influence throughout the world and affect the future of nuclear power development, which, in turn, can exert grave effects on the world's energy supply.

"It is therefore vital, above all, that the nuclear power plants in each country cooperate to improve safety. In this context, although there is already an international network of nuclear power enterprises sharing information, I strongly feel the need to have TQC, which has been painstakingly developed in Japan, shared throughout the world."

NOTES

1 Source is Ian Coyle, Automotive expert, BSI Americas, Inc.
2 Source is a series of online articles on Updates on the ISO 9000's hybrids by Ned Hamson, BRITISH STANDARDS online magazine, Spring 2001.
3 "What Should the Medical Device Industry Do about ISO 9000:2000?" by Amy Zuckerman, BRITISH STANDARDS online magazine, Spring

2001. Content source is Paul Brooks, who is Head of the Notified Body at the British Standards Institution (BSI) United Kingdom office.

4 Material drawn from an article by Peter Aughton – Amerin Consulting Group Pty. Ltd. *The Journal for Quality and Participation*, March 1996.

The State of the Art of Quality

What is the state of the art in quality management? The answer depends on the level of analysis, you select.

If you take the society or community as your unit and if the quality revolution has been ''won,'' then we would expect that most of us would have already experienced a ''vision'' of a total quality community that was proposed in 1990.

''. . . you arrive at the airport, on time and find the place clean and the people friendly. Your baggage is waiting at a clearly marked place very close to the exit to the terminal, on the ground level where the taxis are waiting. As you arrive [at your hotel], the doorman greets you by name and the hotel has the registration form ready for you to sign. All the necessary information has been taken from the computer because the travel agent or your secretary was asked for the details when the reservation was made.''

(Creating a Quality Community, by Kathy Lusk – Technology Exchange Center, Myron Tribus – American Quality and Productivity Institute, and Carole and David Schwinn – Transformation of American Industry Project/Jackson Community College, The Journal for Quality and Participation, *September 1990)*

Now take that same vision, appropriately adapt it, and apply it to:

» places in your community where you shop;
» the average customer's experience with your organization;
» the average supplier's experience with your organization;
» your month in, month out experience with your organization;
» your week in, week out experience in your work group.

Look at your answers – you be the judge: ''Has the quality management revolution been won yet?''

Judged by the standard of that vision, we have not arrived yet. So, how goes the quality movement? We still have a way to go, yes? Before we look at the state of the art, let's briefly revisit a similar assessment made 10 years ago. In the late 1980s and early 1990s, the answers were mixed.

QUALITY'S MIXED RECORD: PAYS HANDSOMELY FOR SOME AND NOT FOR OTHERS

Many companies have quality programs that they judge to be successful:

» A 1992 survey by a team led by Edward Lawler of the University of Southern California showed that nearly two-thirds of the Fortune 1000 in the US had some form of quality management system that used teams and teamwork to improve quality. Survey respondents stated that the involvement of employees in improving quality had been beneficial to the company's performance. The same study showed that, on average, no more than 25 percent of employees were involved in the quality improvement process, however. Later repetitions of the survey and variants of it found the same results – quality and using teams to improve quality worked and paid off. At the same time, the number of people involved in improving quality did not rise.

Many companies "dropped" their quality programs after a few years:

» During the same time period, the US General Accounting Office also did a survey on the impact of quality and employee involvement in quality efforts. Its findings were much the same as found by Lawler's group, except they also found that about two-thirds of organizations surveyed had halted their efforts. Although there is no general study on restarting quality and/or quality team programs, interviews with hundreds of consultants and individuals from those or similar firms show that most did restart their programs, often several times.

What were the experts saying?

Customers in leading industries do not think quality has improved:

» In 1989, Tom Peters said: "My reading of the auto industry evidence, an important leading indicator in the quality movement, is . . . as glum as ever. Consider the data from the latest J. D. Power survey on customers' willingness to recommend auto makes and dealers. Our dealers fared all right, but our cars were shut out – as usual." (Tom Peters, Making It Happen, *The Journal for Quality and Participation*, March, 1989.)

» A year later, Peters noted: "After 10 years of specification-driven quality programs (geared to notions such as mean time between failure and statistical process control charts), my evidence says that we don't get it yet." (Tom Peters, Still Missing After All These Years, *The Journal for Quality and Participation*, March, 1990.)

» In 1989, Phil Crosby said: "My rating of the revolution's progress in installing prevention as the operating philosophy is a 'D.' They seem to think that preventing takes a lot more time than just working things out." (Philip B. Crosby, How goes the quality revolution?, *The Journal for Quality and Participation*, March, 1989.)

[Author's note: The start/stop cycle in formal quality programs ended as ISO 9000 began its steady climb in the number of firms being certified in the mid-1990s. Involving most or all employees in the quality process, however, continues to *not* be the norm among North American, or European firms.]

Japanese firms, however, involved employees in a number of different ways in corporate-wide quality efforts throughout that time and still do; Asian firms that adopted the general Japanese quality model or the Toyota Manufacturing System have done the same.

What about now, where do we stand now? What does recent research show?

Quality is good and it pays off!

» Total quality management (TQM) does have a positive effect on companies' bottom line results, according to research by Professor John Oakland, Dr Mohamed Zairi, and Stephen Letza of Bradford University's European Centre for Total Quality Management who studied the financial results of 29 companies which had implemented TQM for at least five years; their results were above average for their industry median.

Direct worker participation has a strong, positive impact on quality!

» ". . . the strongest impact was on quality, where between 92 and 95% of managers saw a positive impact resulting from different direct participation measures." (Countries included in the study: Denmark, France, Germany, Ireland, Italy, Netherlands, Portugal, Spain, Sweden, and the United Kingdom – From the report by

Keith Sisson for the European Foundation for the Improvement of Living and Working Conditions, entitled *Direct Participation and the Modernization of Work Organization*, ISBN 92-897-0018-1 © European Foundation for the Improvement of Living and Working Conditions, 2000.)

Baldrige Winners Out Perform S&P 500! In the third study of its kind, NIST ''invested'' a hypothetical $1000 in each of the five publicly traded, whole company winners of the Baldrige Quality Award and a percentage of $1000 in the parent companies of nine subsidiary winners.

» NIST found that the group of 16 publicly traded winners – which includes the five whole company winners and the parent companies of winning subsidiaries – outperformed the S&P 500 by about 3 to 1, a 325 percent return on investment compared to a 112 percent return for the S&P 500. NIST studies in 1994 and 1995 also found that Baldrige Award-winning companies outperformed the S&P 500.
» The press release included information about how three winners had fared:
  » At ADAC Laboratories (1996 manufacturing winner), revenue per employee has gone from $175,000 per employee to more than $325,000 per employee in the last several years. Its US market share has increased from 12 percent to 50 percent.
  » In the last five years, Federal Express Corp. (1990 service winner) has increased its operating income by 147 percent while reducing costs per parcel (its primary indicator of efficiency) by 20 percent.
  » Since winning the Baldrige Award in 1988, Globe Metallurgical Inc. (small business winner) has increased revenues by 204 percent and profits by 310 percent. (Press Release: NIST 97-04, Feb. 10, 1997 Contact: Jan Kosko (301) 975-2767 janice.kosko@nist.gov)

WHAT ABOUT ISO 9000? IS IT THE STATE OF THE ART?

Ever since the publication of the ISO 9000 international quality assurance standard in 1987, ISO has been the center of a debate about the standard's efficacy, the cost of registration, and the necessity of similar types of standards.

A number of studies are emerging that purport to measure the effectiveness of ISO 9000. In general, the message is a mixed one; the standard appears to benefit those companies and institutions that earnestly pursue quality improvement, but may have little impact on those using it for marketing purposes only. Even prominent registrars like the British Standards Institution (BSI) warn against expecting ISO 9000 to prove beneficial if the aim is to merely "pass a test."[1]

One of the more prominent studies is being developed by the Carlson School of Management at the University of Minnesota. In brief, the paper investigates what impact the implementation of a new management practice has on organizational performance, specifically looking at organizational implementation of ISO 9000. It states that the evidence from the results of thousands of organizations implementing this standard is mixed.

Some findings show positive benefits, while others show no impact on performance. The paper concludes that whether implementation of a managerial practice, such as ISO 9000, improves organizational performance depends on how the practice is implemented. More success is achieved when the practice is thoroughly assimilated; that is, integrated, externally coordinated, used in daily practice, applied to solving problems, and kept current. However, going beyond the practice's minimum requirements also is necessary. The practice must become a catalyst for rethinking the way an organization does business and a starting point for the introduction of more advanced practices.[2]

THE ONGOING DEBATE ON MANAGEMENT SYSTEM STANDARDS

Besides concern about ISO 9000's efficacy, industry has been concerned that the standard has proved a cash cow for the standard development and registration industries. ISO sparked increased controversy with the subsequent publication of the ISO 14000 environmental management system standard. Alerted to the potential for a "pipeline" of these sorts of standards, with registration schemes attached, industry has rallied and fought back with proposals for management system standards in areas such as occupational health and safety and risk prevention.

But the debate continues as there is market demand in some sectors for these sorts of standards, and the registration world is hardly prepared to drop sure money-makers. The registration community has promoted its own version of an occupational health and safety scheme, for example, along with schemes for data security. The big question is whether these schemes – which are strictly voluntary – warrant international status. Industry fears that once ISO puts its stamp of approval on a given scheme and turns it into an international standard, that standard will become a market requirement.

ISO officials don't care if industry registers to ISO 9000 or any other management system standard as long as global industry groups like ICSCA (Industry Cooperation for Standards and Conformity Assessment) recognize that other groups or companies have needs for such documents. But it's ISO's position that there is a global market demand for management system standards, part of the proof of which is that organizations outside of ISO are selling them. For example, the Australian risk management standard has been adopted in a large way – 17,000 copies sold – by the United Kingdom National Health Service.[3]

What about today? Where does quality stand?

Tom Peters used J. D. Power surveys of the auto industry as good indicators of how seriously people took quality, or how well they were doing with it. How about who dominates in initial quality assessment?

» Japanese quality still dominates vehicle manufacturing! J. D. Power and Associates reports that 11 of the 16 best initial quality vehicles in 2001 were made by Japanese companies. Four of the 16 best were from US vehicle manufacturers; the one remaining vehicle comes from Sweden.

The quality and safety connection

Safety, for many consumers, is a 'quality' issue more important than 'fit and finish.' So?

» The Quality/Safety Scoreboard comparing Ford and Honda: Honda Shines!
  » Recalls issued during 1998 or later: **Ford, Lincoln, Mercury (all models)** – *199* recalls between 1998 and August 2001;

» **Honda/Acura (all models and motorcycles)** – *28* recalls between 1998 and August 2001 (www.safetyalerts.com provided by Safe-T-net, LLC © Copyright 1998–2001.)
» Ford and GM Recall 23 Models of Year 2000 Cars, Trucks, Minivans and SUVs:
  » Washington, DC (Safety Alerts) – The National Highway Traffic Safety Administration (NHTSA) has published the recall of certain model year 2000 Ford and GM vehicles equipped with TRW seat belt buckle assemblies. The buckle bases of these seat belts were not properly heat treated, and therefore do not pass the load bearing requirement of Federal Motor Vehicle Safety Standard No. 209, "Seat Belt Assemblies."

» Many companies have quality programs, they judge to be successful.
» Quality is good and it pays off!
» Direct worker participation has a strong, positive impact on quality!
» Baldrige Winners Out Perform S&P 500!
» Japanese auto firms attain consistent high quality ratings from consumers over the past 20 years.

» Many companies "dropped" their quality programs after a few years.
» Customers in leading industries do not think quality has improved.
» ISO 9000: Some findings show positive benefits, while others show no impact on performance.
» The Quality/Safety Scoreboard comparing Ford and Honda: Honda Shines!
» Ford and GM Recall 23 Models of Year 2000 Cars, Trucks, Minivans, and SUVs.

A mixed record to be sure. There is a significant clue to understanding the meaning behind the "mixed" signals in the note on Ford and GM recalling 23 models of their year 2000 vehicles – "... year 2000 Ford and GM vehicles equipped with TRW seat belt buckle assemblies." TRW, an independent firm, supplies both GM and Ford with seat belt buckles. TRW designs and sells a number of systems and devices to any vehicle manufacturer it can. A few years ago, it was one of the key ABS (automatic braking systems) suppliers to the industry.

Which came first – Team Toyota, Team Honda, or Team Taurus? The point? Japanese manufacturers began quality management during the 1950s with a generations-old assumption that the company and its suppliers were a part of one large team – a *kiritsu*. The success of each and the whole depend on how well they work together. When they began their just-in-time supply and production system in the 1970s it worked well because of years of existing cooperation and joint planning. For the past 10 years or so, each year Honda (Marysville, Ohio) sponsors its own quality conference for all of its suppliers (and invites a few prospective suppliers). Each year, Honda holds an internal competition to select its best quality control circles, which, in addition to being recognized as the best in Ohio, will go to Honda's headquarters in Japan to attend their annual company conference. Toyota and Nissan in the US have similar programs.

When quality management began in the late 1970s and early 1980s at Ford, GM, and Chrysler there was some movement toward the kiritsu model but it was soon abandoned in the name of cost savings or efficiency. Ford, early on, offered free SPC and quality circle training to its first-tier suppliers. Cincinnati Milacron, a supplier of machine tools, and a number of other firms influenced by the automakers did likewise. By 1985–86, suppliers were "required" to be certified as meeting the individual company's quality standard. Not long after, US automakers supported the creation of a unified industry standard QS 9000, which drew heavily from the just issued ISO 9000.

What North American and European managers did not understand fully then or now is that quality management stands or falls on four pillars: a systems perspective, process management, statistical analysis and control, and a group orientation. When the Japanese talked about the group and group work, the listening North Americans and Europeans, even when they heard and translated correctly, "saw" or "understood" group as team and teamwork; and team and teamwork understood through their own historical and cultural perspectives. European and North American firms will not be able to match the Japanese manufacturers in whole system application of quality principles until promotions and recognition are commonplace for being a good group member or a member of a high-performing group that supports other groups, etc.

Toyota, Honda, Nissan, Sony, Panasonic, etc. are state of the art in understanding and using the type of group work required to support system-wide quality management.

An indirect measure of how North American and European firms differ from Japanese firms on this group dimension of quality management is the current popularity of Six Sigma and the now "discarded" or old program, reengineering. Both approaches took the usual mix of quality methods that lent themselves to studying and improving processes that crossed departmental boundaries and packaged them for use by specialist teams or managers. Specialists and managers in the European and North American management systems are measured, rewarded, and promoted in comparison to whether they outperformed other specialists or managers. In quality programs that emphasized teamwork, they had no way to achieve individual recognition. The problem in systems based on individual achievement rather than group achievement was to find an appropriate "role" for managers and supervisors. Six Sigma, with its "Black Belts" (expert, or master level), gives managers and specialists an individual role for which they can be measured against each other and rewarded. And while the training of these managers in quality methods represents an advance over past practices, it cannot achieve the same level of organizational effectiveness or benefits as that achieved by the typical firm using the "whole" Toyota Management System.

WHAT ABOUT STATE OF THE ART IN A COMPLETE QUALITY MANAGEMENT SYSTEM?

The nod, again, has to go to firms such as Toyota, Honda, Nissan, Sony, Panasonic, etc. The reason is that when a Japanese firm adds a new quality tool, it does not generally discard or downplay the tools that had been in use. For example, when a Honda team reports on their improvement project, they report which tools were used and why other tools were not used.

Most North American firms and, to a large extent, European firms as well, have approached quality management as they have other advances in management and technology, in a programed manner.

When a new program is being pushed, the old program is either downplayed, discarded wholesale, or euphemistically said to no longer be special and either the "way we do business" or still a part of what can be used voluntarily.

The Japanese began with seven basic quality tools: flowcharting, check sheets, Pareto diagrams, cause and effect diagrams, control charts, scatter diagrams, and histograms were used by individuals and quality control circles. They are all still in use.

Then they added the seven new management and planning tools: the affinity diagram, the interrelationship diagram, the tree diagram, the matrix diagram, the prioritization matrix, the process decision program chart, and the activity network diagram.

How have US firms fared in using the seven basic tools? A 1990 North American study of which tools were being used and how often they were being used demonstrated that use of the seven basic tools is far from uniform:

1 flowcharting (70 percent);
2 cause and effect diagrams (67 percent);
3 Pareto diagrams (63 percent);
4 control charts (48 percent);
5 scatter diagrams (36 percent).

An Australian researcher who had also surveyed several hundred quality managers in the US and in Europe found a similar spread and selective use of the tools. Selective use of quality tools in North America has not changed.

The only US firm we know of that will soon reach the same state of the art status as most Japanese manufacturers is UICI Insurance in Fort Worth, Texas. The reason is that the person guiding the now two-year-old quality process, Pat Townsend, began it with the agreement of its CEO that all employees, including the CEO, would be trained in quality methods, be evaluated for their quality improvement involvement and performance, and have several means to participate in the improvement process. If the length of time it takes to launch a quality management system and achieve 100 percent involvement is a part of measuring state of the art, UICI would be at the leading edge, since the system was planned, designed and implemented in 12 months – and on day one, there was 100 percent participation.

CHALLENGES, ISSUES, AND THE FUTURE FOR QUALITY AND QUALITY MANAGEMENT

ISO 9000 challenges

ISO 9000 will reduce the start and stop nature of quality programs in North America and Europe and it will increase the raw number of firms that have a formal quality management system in place.

As ISO 9000 and its industry-specific derivatives are even more widely accepted and implemented, the general state of the art in quality management will be advanced, at least in the sense that the ability of firms to treat quality as an add-on or a budget area with less priority than others will be restricted. And as long as customers "require" firms to be ISO 9000 registered, starting and stopping a formal quality program will no longer be an option. This "restriction" may well be a significant reason for tension and resistance toward ISO 9000 discussed below.

Industry is pushing self-declaration

On some occasions, such as several attempts in the late 1990s and in 2000 to have ISO develop a standard for occupational health and safety, groups like ICSCA have rallied their members – mainly multinational companies in the high-tech, aerospace, telecommunications, and automotive/heavy equipment fields – to fight within the ISO system. Besides literally stalling production of management system standards, ICSCA is promoting self-declaration to standards like ISO 9000. This is called supplier's self-declaration of conformity assessment (SDOC), and it means that the third-party auditor – or registrar – is then eliminated from the process.

A number of ICSCA companies, including Siemens and Hewlett-Packard, have flirted with the SDOC approach, though none have publicly announced they are dropping their ISO 9000 registration programs. Ironically, some companies who are fighting against multiple registrations and management system standards also recognize that this approach may actually be easier and require less work than the SDOC approach. With self-declaration, a company has to provide a huge amount of documentation to prove to the world that it is meeting quality criteria of the sort that ISO 9000 and other quality programs promote.

Guido Guertler, Head of Standards and Regulation, Siemens, believes that, "Over the next 10 years it's clear that the market will make a much better distinction between good brand name companies and others. The good brands will not need to show third-party certification. Good companies will have the tendency to drop ISO 9000 third-party certification, which doesn't mean not to practice it. But the certification is of limited value. What will happen is that an increasing number of companies will practice self-assessment according to Malcolm Baldrige, EFQM (European Quality Award), and others' models, and show self-assessment to the public and customers."[4]

In fact, SDOC has been legally established in Australia, according to ICSCA officials. Efficient market surveillance has been developed to back up the process, and is considered key to making SDOC work. Penalties are awarded to those found not to be in compliance.

Keeping tests and audits to a minimum

Groups like ICSCA and the International Accreditation Forum (IAF) have alerted both the registration industry and bodies like the World Trade Organization (WTO) to their concern to keep audits to standards in the ISO 9000 family to a minimum, along with raising concerns about the proliferation of product testing being imposed by industries, countries, and regional economic blocks worldwide. A relatively new group of power-house international registrars – Partners in World Safety – is working to promote "one-stop testing," as well.

A number of registrars, many of whom belong to the Independent Association of Accredited Registrars, are also exploring conducting streamlined registrations. Auditors are being trained at places like BSI to test for several standards in the ISO 9000 community at the same time. Some combinations include joint audits for ISO 9000 and ISO 14000 or ISO 9000 and QS-9000.

What will the future bring for ISO 9000?

Officials at ISO don't see any end in sight, for the moment, in the development of ISO 9000 hybrids. And when industry wants an international version of one of those hybrids, they say they'll help them develop it. In the long run, they believe that ISO 9000 will be the glue that pulls all the hybrids together – the underlying quality base that offers a structure for quality management whether the realm is medical devices or automotives. And they believe that the standard provides corporate cohesion that wouldn't be there without it, which is particularly important in global operations.

As for the backlash against management system standards, they say they'll be developed when there's a market demand. For example, groups like ICSCA helped squash a risk management standard in ISO. An Australian standards body developed a risk management standard and it's been a hot seller.[5]

THE FUTURE AND ISSUES FOR QUALITY MANAGEMENT AS A WHOLE

Firms that are depending on Six Sigma or some similar "branded" quality approach that depends on managers or "specialists" for quality improvement will have to re-involve the rest of their employees to reach the same levels of quality management achievement as Toyota or Honda.

Firms that are depending on ISO 9000 registration of their suppliers to improve their supply chain management, or hoping that it will do so, will be disappointed in short order. Since forming formal versions of Japanese *kiritsu* might have anti-competitive implications, American firms, in particular, will have to continue working hard to improve how they work with their "partner" suppliers. Returning to a system of simply throwing "RFPs" over the wall for all-against-all bidding is not a real choice when faced with competing against firms working together as a group.

Individual firms that wish to achieve the state of the art level of Toyota in overall quality management will have to continue working on how to measure and reward group work, rather than simply add, as many have done, quality measures to managers' performance ratings. These firms will have to devise ways to measure and reward the work of groups and how well individuals contribute to the success of their group. This does not mean that rewarding individual contributions should end, for it is an important ingredient in supporting individual creativity and innovation.

Firms that have just entered the quality arena because they "had" to be ISO certified, or thought that ISO 9000 and the package available would give them Toyota-quality, will soon learn that there is a lot more to quality management and improvement than they imagined. Since many of these firms are smaller, they will create a market to deliver training and quality support systems that "fit" their size and budget. Most training and systems available today were designed with the Fortune 1000 in mind. Even though an unintended consequence, this market force will fuel a broad advance in quality for the average customer or consumer.

NOTES

1 Source is Reg Blake, Vice President of Development, BSI Americas from "ISO 9000: Leverage ISO 9000 for Added Value and Bottom-Line Benefits, *Fortune* magazine, May 11, 1998.
2 Jim McCabe, staff member at the American National Standards Institute (ANSI), summary of the Minnesota study.
3 Mike Smith, ISO Head of Standards, ISO, from *Standards, Technology and Global Trends*, Amy Zuckerman, 2000, A – Z International Associates, Amherst, MA.
4 Guido Guertler, Head of Standards and Regulation, Siemens, from *Standards, Technology and Global Trends*, Amy Zuckerman, 2000, A – Z International Associates, Amherst, MA.
5 Source is Mike Smith, head of standards, ISO, from an interview with Amy Zuckerman, Spring 2001.

Quality in Practice: Case Studies

» In the US: Three simple tools with big results
» In the United Kingdom: Prudential Assurance Company
» In the US: Solectron Technology
» In India: Sundaram-Clayton
» The Deming Prize criteria

[Authors' note: Each of the following case studies represents a "time-less" set of best practices during a specific slice of time. (The practices and methods discussed may or may not be representative of present practices in the organization.) Each demonstrates the potential benefits for your organization of applying the tools or methods discussed to your particular mix of employees, customers, and suppliers, under existing market or societal conditions.]

UNITED STATES: THREE SIMPLE TOOLS WITH BIG RESULTS

The quality improvement process at Delco Remy (now Delphi Automotive Systems) during the late 1980s and early 1990s was driven by GM's corporate commitment to quality through its Quality Network, but specifically, the permanent loss of jobs in a town where Delco Remy was a major employer drove the operations side of labor and management working together on improving quality of product, thereby providing greater job security.

In August of 1987, this plant's personnel department began a quality effort that used:

1 Phil Crosby's basic tools: knowing and satisfying your customer's requirements, the cost of quality, and the price of non-conformance;
2 flowcharting and doing a through-put analysis of all tasks;
3 doing a value-added analysis of all the steps detailed in the flowcharts.

Odail Thorns, Jr., the department's head, said that the through-put analysis alone helped each unit in the department to fully document what it takes to do every job. That, in turn, helped people find which steps can be eliminated or combined and assists the unit in carrying out critical functions when an employee is on vacation or out due to illness.

The introduction of each method was straightforward and not all that complex. The 70 or so employees all received training in Crosby's basic tools in a one-day session led by Department head Thorns.

Following that training, each group had one month to interview and determine the key requirements of their customers for their output.

The department's sense of its mission and how it related to helping the entire organization meet its goals was uncanny. Using the process of interviewing and surveying customers had taught each unit where they fit in making Delco Remy run smoothly.

Then all employees were trained in basic flowcharting and asked to have all their individual and group tasks charted over the next six months.

When that was completed a through-put and value-added analysis was done with an eye for improvements that would improve their productivity and enable them to continue to meet their customer's requirements.

The ability to not let anything lie waiting is one of the chief objects of the through-put job analysis that each employee is completing in this personnel department. The other is to identify inefficiencies and ways to better serve customers inside and outside of the department.

The department's labor relations unit offers an example of what this process accomplished in finances and in attitudes.

In an area traditionally rife with suspicion and conflict, this unit tracked the number of grievances by type and publicly posted it. Too many grievances in any particular area became a price of non-conformance for them. Prior to the decision to work with labor and to focus on quality, tracking, and posting the numbers of grievances was unthinkable, because the numbers could be used as weapons for either side.

An upward spike in the number of grievances over a particular contract paragraph indicated to them that a problem-solving process was needed. When this occurred last year, the unit found that the spike was due to a lack of training for shop committee people and first-line supervisors new to their positions. The response was to design, with union representatives, a short course on how to apply a particular paragraph. The reduced number of grievances meant more time working than preparing for and attending grievance meetings.

Timeline

» **August 1987**: The department's quality program was begun.
  » People were trained in how to identify and interview customers regarding their requirements.
  » People were given basic training in determining their cost of quality and price of non-conformance to customers' requirements.

» People were asked after this half-day training to interview all their customers within one month and agree on the requirements that they were expected to meet.

» Individuals and groups began to modify/improve processes immediately to meet customers' requirements.

» **September 1987**: At the beginning of the second month sub-units of the department began publicly posting their tracking of meeting their customers' requirements, their cost of quality, their price of non-conformance and any improvements made.

» **October 1987**: Department employees were all given basic training in constructing flowcharts of each of their assigned tasks. They were given six months to completely chart all tasks.

» **March 1988**: Training in through-put analysis (value-adding/non-value-adding) to enable individuals and groups to determine when, where, and how non-value-adding tasks and steps might be subtracted from their processes based on re-interviewing customers, where necessary. Six months were allotted to this departmental task.

Key lessons/insights

» When support or administrative departments focus on knowing and meeting their customer requirements, operations and management employees can then better focus on their primary work.

» Interviewing customers to determine their requirements does much more than establish what those requirements are. It lays the groundwork for improved communications of all types.

Those doing the interviewing better learn how and where they "fit" in the organization – what their contribution to the organization is.

UNITED KINGDOM: PRUDENTIAL ASSURANCE COMPANY

Extensive market research showed that the company needed to improve performance in terms both of customer service and of productivity. It also showed that their current cost base and staffing levels were not sustainable.

Their first step was to launch a TQM program aimed at active participation (teamwork) as well as the use of individual judgment and initiative.

The program (Way of Life) began by translating the company's mission statement into a set of principles and values – Way of Life statements. To keep these principles and values linked with business objectives, management established a set of key business indicators (KBIs) which would focus the program on the crucial key business drivers:

Efficiency (doing things right the first time) ... effectiveness (doing the right things)

Their one-year departmental plans, developed as a mechanism for moving the TQM program forward, closely reflected the overall business plan. Departmental targets were linked with key business indicators and individual staff objectives, and accountability became the responsibility of senior managers, department managers, and supervisors, who were to link personal development plans with both business targets and the quality initiative.

The business planning process became indivisible from the quality improvement process, and the way to achieve business targets was through the quality initiative, not simply by working harder. Even though improving customer satisfaction was a key goal, at first work groups chose most often to work on cost-cutting and efficiency activities because they were easier to measure.

A major breakthrough was a reassessment of the way in which they measured customer satisfaction. The earlier customer program had focused on improving service that the customer did not actually see or was terribly interested in. There was a need to change to what the customer actually experienced.

The Customer Experience Research project identified a series of key transactions in customer priority order. The customer priority research showed that claims and payments should be the company's top priority, followed by the way it handles complaints. Processing new business came further down the list when viewed from their customers' perspective.

The research project also included customer satisfaction surveys designed to give feedback on a range of measures, including professionalism, presentation, knowledge base, politeness, telephone manner, accessibility, clarity of documentation, and incidence of jargon. They also extended the range of the speed and accuracy audits, introduced telephone audits, and instituted quantitative and qualitative customer feedback surveys.

Analysis of the data captured helped Life Administration to identify the techniques which they should use to assess more accurately customer satisfaction levels. Based on this information, the company reengineered its processes so that they reflect the customer's experience, representing a 180-degree shift in the company's perspective.

Timeline

» **December 1989**: Prudential Assurance business plan defined key business targets and activities for the next three years.
  » Over a six-week period, 260 staff from board level to supervisors were trained in a cascading fashion.
  » Following this, supervisors were trained in team leadership and in how to train their teams in TQM.
  » Finally, line employees received their training in teamwork and quality improvement from their supervisors.
» **1991**: Prudential Assurance wins the UK's Department of Employment and Training award.
» **1992**: Prudential Assurance wins the UK's Department of Employment and Training award.
» **1992**: Prudential Assurance's Industrial Branch is certified by BSI as meeting the BS5750 quality standard (forerunner of ISO 9000).

Key lessons/insights

» When companies are able to take a step back and look at themselves from their customer's perspective, it enables them to reorient their priorities to be in line with those of the customer, rather than those the company "assume" are important. Prudential Assurance used survey and priority research.[1]
» Process improvements and key business indicators derived from actual customer preferences enable companies such as Prudential

to spend time and budget on factors that improve customer satisfaction and retention, as well as additional sales. At the same time, such a company can reduce time and funds spent on items of less importance to the customer.[2]

PRUDENTIAL ASSURANCE AND ITS BS5750 CERTIFICATION – WHY AND HOW?
Benefits of certification

The insurance industry in the UK is so strictly regulated by legislation that some form of quality assurance has always existed. Thus, there were no commercial pressures on Prudential to adopt the standard, and only a limited marketing benefit – most of the end-users of insurance products have never heard of it. The benefits lay in an entirely different direction:

1 The emphasis on processes and inputs provides an additional degree of control over the business at a time when costs are increasingly under the spotlight.
2 It imposes a discipline on managers and ensures that they fulfill their obligations as defined in their personal objectives.
3 It helps staff to review the highly complex documentation which accompanies processing systems and to identify opportunities to improve it.

UNITED STATES: A SOLECTRON TEAM FROM SOLECTRON TECHNOLOGY, CHARLOTTE, NC, USES KAIZEN BLITZ PROCESS TO QUICKLY RESPOND TO CUSTOMER COMPLAINTS

Lucent Technologies, a customer of Solectron, was not satisfied with the defects showing up in printed-circuit board hardware. The director of operations asked Jeff Portada, in that area, if he thought one of his teams could solve the problem – and in a hurry. Portada said that the team would love to use the Kaizen blitz process, which is a one-week process that uses a lean manufacturing tool to try to reduce waste and improve quality.

They were given the go-ahead to give it a try. The team defined their task simply – to redefine the process and layout for a printed-circuit board hardware assembly area. The end result?

» A 46% productivity improvement.
» A 33% reduction in the amount of floor space needed for the activity.
» A 50% reduction in the incidence of rejects.

As a company, Solectron has applied for the national quality award in the US (Malcolm Baldrige National Quality Award) twice – and won it twice. The company has used state quality awards and award processes of professional associations as "outside" measurement or testing of the "quality" of the quality processes and teamwork at each of their sites and as incentive to the organization and its employees to continuously improve their work, satisfy customers, and improve the bottom line for the company.

Kaizen blitzing

The start: The team developed a project charter (problem statement) to narrow the scope of what they would work on in the week they had to begin and finish the project. Their key guide was to make improvements that improved Solectron's bottom line and satisfied the needs of their customer.

The Hardware Assembly Kaizen Team, the Solectron team, was made up of 15 people drawn from different levels and different operations in the organization. They used several tools very effectively. Among them were spaghetti diagrams, process mapping, and gripe interviews. Through this process, the team uncovered root causes, areas to reduce waste, and opportunities to begin improvements.

The team spent about 50 percent of the 8–10 hours a day devoted to the project on the manufacturing floor. That enabled them to quickly see and address problems.

What is not finished and implemented within the week is included in a 30-day action plan. The team tracks the action plan being implemented by people in the affected area.

This particular Solectron Kaizen Blitz team entered the national team excellence process of the Association for Quality and Participation in the US. They were awarded a bronze for third place against stiff competition from 17 other teams. They were supported by a facilitator who works with a number of different types of improvement teams at Solectron. Solectron has been using a variety of team-based and project-based problem solving and prevention for more than ten years.

Timeline

» One work week:
  » Day one: Define and narrow scope, decide what tools will be used to gather and analyze data, begin collecting information about the problem, as well as suggestions for solutions as they interview people.
  » Day two: Continue collecting data and suggestions, analyze data as it comes in and implement corrections or changes consistent with the goals or team charter.
  » Day three: Continue collecting data and suggestions, analyze data as it comes in and implement corrections or changes consistent with the goals or team charter.
  » Day four: Summarize data and suggestions into the overall action plan that has been in the process of implementation during the week.
  » Day five: Implement corrections or changes consistent with the goals or team charter that have not yet been implemented and write up the whole process. Items that must still be implemented are scheduled for a 30-day action plan that the team will track. Items that need more than one week's verification are included in the 30-day action plan for either changes or final acceptance.

Key insights

» Quality improvement processes can begin and end quickly.
» A team approach that draws in people experienced in quality methods and teamwork.
» Corporate support for the team and quality approaches throughout the organization support the spread of best practices and the belief that groups can "test" out, on their own initiative, new approaches that promise to improve the satisfaction of customers, the company's bottom line and the work of Solectron employees.

INDIA:SUNDARAM-CLAYTON OF INDIA WINS JAPAN'S 1999 DEMING PRIZE

Sundaram-Clayton, a Chennai (Madras), India-based manufacturer of air-brake systems and castings, has used company-wide quality control as a significant means of supporting the company's drive to be competitive in its home market and ultimately in the international automobile and truck market.

This firm, as was the case of most other Indian firms, had no incentive to be competitive for some 30 years (1960–1990), as the Indian market was protected by a licensing system. Since 1990, however, Indian companies have had to relearn how to be competitive internally and on the world market. The total quality strategy of this firm achieved "world class" standards when it won Japan's Deming Prize in 1999. The firm is only the fourth non-Japanese firm to win the Deming Prize since it was established in 1951 and expanded to include non-Japanese firms in 1985.[3]

JUSE's rigorous quality audit tests a company on 10 parameters that, between them, envelop each and every activity of a company. The theme that is tested across every operation is the ability of a company to use statistics-driven quality-control mechanisms to produce – consistently, economically, and reliably – a product or service that meets the customer's requirement in every possible manner – time after time after time.

Bottom-line results of Sundaram-Clayton's total quality movement during the five years between 1992–93 and 1997–98 were as follows.

» Sales grew at an average rate of 35 percent per annum between 1992–93 and 1996–97, although they shrank by 25 percent in 1997–98 on account of the recession in the automobile industry.

» The average growth in net profits in those four years was 83 percent per annum – it fell back by 35 percent during the 1997–98 recession in the automobile industry.

» Internally, its performance improved consistently, with turnover per employee rising by an average of 18 percent a year, and gross value added climbing by an average of 12 percent per annum.

SUNDARAM-CLAYTON'S QUALITY POLICY

"Sundaram-Clayton will deliver a level of quality that totally meets customer expectations. This customer satisfaction will be obtained by supplying products of the right quality, at the right time, and at the right place. Total employee involvement and continuous improvement in every sphere of activity will be the twin supports on which Sundaram-Clayton quality will stand."

Examples of how Sundaram-Clayton uses quality management to "manage" the firm are given below.

Policy deployment

Policy deployment spells out the objectives of all levels of employees in the organization, from the CEO – for the next five years – down to the machine-operator – for the next 30 minutes.

The company selects the critical issues three months ahead of each new financial year using Deming's PDSA cycle: Plan – Do – Study – Act. The three most important issues are picked for focus, and communicated to everybody in the company as Managing Points and Checking Points. Total quality control (TQC) tools are used to measure progress once the objective has been defined.

» The president's Managing Points – which flow from his objectives – become the Checking Points for the manager immediately under him.
» The sales target of the head of marketing is his Managing Point – and is split into Checking Points under segment sales and territory sales.

By vertically connecting Managing and Checking Points, Sundaram-Clayton structures itself to single-mindedly pursue its stated policy objective for the year. And, applying data-driven company-wide quality control (CWQC), the progress is depicted on charts, with deviations showing up as red lines – the recurrence of which kick off problem-solving cycles.

Quality in daily work

Sundaram-Clayton uses statistical quality control (SQC) across departments and functions. Every machine on Sundaram-Clayton's shop floor has its own daily work-management system through which its operators meet quality and hourly production goals.

When there is a deviation from the daily schedule, the cause is analyzed and acted upon immediately. This dramatically lowers nonconformity.

Product design

A cross-functional team – representing engineering, marketing, production, purchase, and R&D – forms the product development team. First, data is collected from the customer by this cross-functional team. A product development committee examines issues like the life expectancy of the product, production volume, growth, target cost, and the availability of in-house competency to meet the requirement. If the design is satisfactory, a rapid prototyping of the product is done. This is then tested and validated for manufacture.

As the product design team is getting its specifications together, another part of the team begins work on the supply chain, getting the components-base ready. By the time the customer approves the design and the first prototype is made, suppliers too are ready.

This approach enabled Sundaram-Clayton to reduce its new-product development time from between 24–30 months to between 12–14 months.

Venu Srinivasan, CEO, Sundaram-Clayton, on what a target like vying for the Deming Prize did for his organization, said: "I thought that the Prize would tell our people that they have achieved something. And that sense of achievement is important because I know that while the company is continuously moving in the right direction, people need to know that; they need to take home that message. The Deming Prize has brought kudos to each employee who has put in 10 years of hard work. He can go back and tell his family: 'You've been wondering why I've been away day and night working for the company, but now you know. We are a company of a different quality. We are up there. We are the elite.'"

Timeline

» **1986**: Sundaram-Clayton began its formal quality management process when its managers were taught about TQC, first by Yoshio Kondo in 1986, and, from 1989 onwards, under the tutelage of Washio and Tsuda.
  » The firm used a variety of award processes as means to both measure and give recognition of the firm's quality progress.
» **1989**: It won the Confederation of Indian Industry's (CII) Quality Circle award, followed, in 1990, by awards from the Quality Circle Federation of India.
» **1995**: CEO Srinivasan challenged his team to begin the process for entering and winning the Deming Prize (please see box on the Deming Prize Criteria).
» They won the 1999 Deming Prize.

Key insights

» External measures or competitions such as the Deming Prize not only act as markers of a company's progress, but significantly improve and sustain morale and employee satisfaction. They do this by giving both meaning and recognition to both team and individual work contributions by employees.
» The quality deployment process demonstrates concretely how quality and quality management support are integral to the strategy of the firm and the business goals of its officers and employees.[4]

THE DEMING PRIZE CRITERIA

The Deming Prize is, of course, named after W. Edwards Deming, one of the pioneers of the quality movement, who first gained recognition in his work with post-World War II Japan. The Deming Prize criteria can be used as a guide for obtaining process and organizational excellence. Each area deals with one facet of the process quality equation.

1.0 Policy
1.1 Policies pursued for management, quality, and quality control

1.2 Method of establishing policies
1.3 Justifiability and consistency of policies
1.4 Utilization of statistical methods
1.5 Transmission and diffusion of policies
1.6 Review of policies and the results achieved
1.7 Relationship between policies and long- and short-term planning
2.0 Organization and its management
2.1 Explicitness of the scopes of authority and responsibility
2.2 Appropriateness of delegations of authority
2.3 Interdivisional cooperation
2.4 Committees and their activities
2.5 Utilization of staff
2.6 Utilization of quality control circles
2.7 Quality control diagnosis
3.0 Education and dissemination
3.1 Education programs and results
3.2 Quality and control consciousness, degrees of understanding of quality control
3.3 Teaching and extent of dissemination of statistical concepts and methods
3.4 Grasp of the effectiveness of quality control
3.5 Education of related entities: contractors and vendors
3.6 Quality control circle activities
3.7 System of suggesting ways of improvements and its actual conditions
4.0 Collection, dissemination and use of information on quality
4.1 Collection of external information
4.2 Transmission of information between divisions
4.3 Speed of information transmission
4.4 Data processing, statistical analysis of information, and use of results
5.0 Analysis
5.1 Selection of key problems and themes
5.2 Propriety of the analytical approach
5.3 Utilization of statistical methods

5.4 Linkage with proper technology

5.5 Quality analysis, process analysis

5.6 Utilization of analytical results

5.7 Assertiveness of improvement suggestions

6.0 Standardization

6.1 Systematization of standards

6.2 Method of establishing, revising, and abolishing standards

6.3 Outcome of the establishment, revision, or abolition of standards

6.4 Contents of the standards

6.5 Utilization of statistical methods

6.6 Accumulation of technology

6.7 Utilization of standards

7.0 Control

7.1 Systems for the control of quality and related cost

7.2 Control items and control points

7.3 Utilization of such statistical control methods as control charts

7.4 Contribution to performance of Quality Control circle activities

7.5 Actual conditions of control activities

7.6 State of matters under control

8.0 Quality assurance

8.1 Procedure for the development of new products and services

8.2 Safety and immunity from product liability

8.3 Process design, process analysis, and process improvement

8.4 Process capability

8.5 Instrumentation

8.6 Equipment maintenance and control of purchases

8.7 Quality assurance system and its audit

8.8 Utilization of statistical methods

8.9 Evaluation and audit of quality

8.10 Actual state of quality assurance

9.0 Results

9.1 Measurement of results

9.2 Substantive results in quality, services, and delivery time, cost

9.3 Intangible results

NOTES

1 Quality Function Deployment – described elsewhere in this book – is a tool that works well to design or redesign a service or product around real customer preferences and requirements, and in order of importance. A number of companies have successfully used QFD not only to determine what is really important to customers but to reduce their costs by not "engineering in" quality that the customer has no interest in and that does not affect the performance or perceived value of the product or service.

2 Source of information: Stephen Tanner – *Prudential Assurance Company Journal for Quality and Participation*, December 1994

3 Note on the Deming Prize and non-Japanese competitors: The three other non-Japanese winning companies are: Florida Power & Light, which won the Deming Prize; AT&T's Power Systems Division; and Philips's Taiwan unit.

4 Drawn from interviews by R. Sridharan of Living Media India Ltd.

Key Concepts and Thinkers of Quality and Quality Management

» Definitively defining quality
» The customer defined
» Getting to what's important from the customers
  » Crosby, Deming, and Juran compared
» The keys to the people side of quality
  » Improving a task
  » Improving a process
» ISO 9000 and employee participation
» Pulling the people part all together
» Key people in ISO 9000

DEFINITIVELY DEFINING QUALITY

The key concepts that define quality and quality management begin with its definition. This definition from the website of the International Standards Organization works quite well for most uses:

> "... the standardized definition of 'quality' in ISO 9000 refers to all those features of a product (or service) which are required by the customer.
>
> 'Quality management' means what the organization does to ensure that its products conform to the customer's requirements."
>
> *(Source: http://www.iso.ch/iso/en/iso9000-14000/tour/plain.html)*

The customer defined

The definition of customer most commonly begins with the point of sale purchaser. If the definition of customer began and ended there, however, many more companies would be having difficulties staying in business today. The expanded definition of customer can and does include:

» the employee to whom you pass your work;
» the point of sales purchaser, other end users;
» those impacted by the end users' use of your product (safety and environmental issues, for example);
» the stock holder, if it is a publicly owned firm (the citizen, if it is a government agency).

[Author's note: This expanded definition of the "customer" whose requirements must be considered and met makes clear why ISO 14000 (systematic management of environmental concerns and factors) was built on a foundation similar to that of ISO 9000. ISO 14000, in a sense, helps an organization meet the community's requirements for environmental security from negative impacts from the company's manufacturing and/or service processes or the use of its products or services. In like fashion, if in the future an international standard is established for occupational health and safety management, it would be crafted in a manner similar to ISO 9000 and 14000 and would help an organization meet the requirements of its employees.]

GETTING TO WHAT'S IMPORTANT FROM THE CUSTOMER'S PERSPECTIVE

The key to meeting the requirements of the "customer" is actually rather simple, but as the Prudential Assurance case noted, can still be missed, even by those to whom quality, accuracy, and productivity are the aims of the system.

Every time I heard someone ask the late Phil Crosby, "How do you know what the requirements are or if you've met them?" Crosby would smile and say: "Ask them and they will tell you." If you recall the Prudential case, the company had a great number of items being measured to indicate success or quality. The trouble was, they were not the things that the customer cared about, or, at least, cared about most. So the key means to meeting your requirements is asking the customer what they are. And if you are really advanced in your quality thinking, as the Japanese experts would advise, you will have moved to preventing error or poor quality in the customer's eyes. One of the most important quality methods available, though not the most used, is what is called quality function deployment (QFD). In QFD, you build in talking with the customer as you design and/or improve a product or service. QFD then takes customer requirements and transforms them into technical requirements and processes that can be carried through each stage of the production or service process. A ranking of the importance of features, functions, and capabilities is also a key part of the QFD process.

The Mark Graham Brown article on service QFD listed in the resources section notes that without a QFD analysis, you might have thought that being open certain hours with added staff costs was necessary to successfully meet the customer's requirements in comparison to a competitor. But using the QFD process – talking with potential or existing customers – to redesign your service process shows you that this matters less to the customer than another less costly aspect of the service. Building in the customer's voice not only assures meeting the correct requirements, it may well mean reducing unnecessary costs.

Table 8.1, comparing the capsulated quality systems of Crosby, Deming, and Juran, will help take us through the major concepts involved in quality and quality management.

Table 8.1 Crosby, Deming, and Juran compared. (Source: Three paths, one journey, Steve Gibbons – RSM McGladrey, Inc., *Journal for Quality and Participation*, October/November 1994.)

Philip B. Crosby	W. Edwards Deming	Joseph M. Juran
Quality is conformance to requirements	*Quality is continuous improvement through reduced variation*	*Quality is fitness for use*
The Four Absolutes of Quality Management:	**The Seven Deadly Diseases:**	**The Quality Trilogy:**
1 The definition of quality is conformance to requirements	1 Lack of constancy of purpose	1 Quality improvement
2 The system of quality is prevention	2 Emphasizing short-term profits and immediate dividends	2 Quality planning
3 The performance standard is zero defects	3 Evaluation of performance, merit rating or annual review	3 Quality control
4 The measurement of quality is the price of non-conformance	4 Mobility of top management	**Ten-Step Quality Improvement Process:**
Fourteen-Step Quality Improvement Plan:	5 Running a company only on visible figures	1 Build awareness of the need and opportunity for improvement
1 Management commitment is defined, created, and exhibited	6 Excessive medical costs	2 Set goals for improvement
2 Quality improvement team is formed	7 Excessive costs of warranty fueled by lawyers on contingency fees	3 Organize to reach the goals

Table 8.1 (*Continued*).

Philip B. Crosby	W. Edwards Deming	Joseph M. Juran
3 Measurement to determine areas for improvement	**The Fourteen Points:**	4 Provide training throughout the organization
4 Cost of quality measures are developed as a stimulus	1 Create constancy of purpose for improvement of product and service	5 Carry out projects to solve problems
5 Quality awareness is created in everyone	2 Adopt the new philosophy	6 Report progress
6 Corrective action is taken on problems previously identified	3 Cease dependence on mass inspection	7 Give recognition
7 Zero defects planning	4 End the practice of awarding business on price tag alone	8 Communicate results
8 Employee education of all employees in the company	5 Improve constantly and forever the system of production and service	9 Keep score
9 Zero defects day is held to let all employees know there has been a change	6 Institute training on the job	10 Maintain momentum by making annual improvement part of the regular systems and processes of the company
10 Goal setting for individuals and groups	7 Institute leadership	
11 Error cause removal by employees sharing with management the obstacles they face in attaining goals	8 Drive out fear	
12 Recognition for those who participated	9 Break down barriers between staff areas	

(*continued overleaf*)

Table 8.1 (*Continued*).

Philip B. Crosby	W. Edwards Deming	Joseph M. Juran
13 Quality councils to communicate regularly	10 Eliminate slogans, exhortations, and targets for the workforce	
14 Do it all over again to emphasize quality improvement never ends	11a Eliminate numerical quotas for the workforce	
	11b Eliminate numerical goals for people in management	
	12 Remove barriers to pride of workmanship	
	13 Encourage education and self-improvement for everyone	
	14 Take action to accomplish the transformation	

Many people think and believe that quality management is about the technical, or "hard" side of the business or achieving goals. They point to measurement systems, statistical tools, and automated quality control systems. Those same people often refer to the "other" side of quality management – the people side – as the "soft" side. Let us examine that briefly since it takes us to the next important concept of quality and quality management.

Deming says that, "Quality is improved in three ways:

» through innovation in design of a product or service;
» through innovation in processes; and
» through improvement of existing processes."

How are those improvements brought about? Look at the table comparing Crosby, Deming, and Juran and you will see that numbers 5 through 14 of Deming's 14 points deal with how people do their work, are managed, or led. Number 2 and then 5 through 14 of Crosby's 14 steps of quality all deal with how people do their work, are managed, or led. All 10 of Dr Juran's quality improvement steps deal with how people do their work, are managed, or led. So it seems that one of the key concepts in quality is supporting, managing, and leading people.

When Dr Feigenbaum, also one of the founders of modern quality, was asked in 1996, "What are good managers doing?", he replied: "Using the knowledge, skills and attitudes of every man and woman in the organization, encouraging and supporting the freedom to innovate, supporting solving problems democratically, valuing the sense of teamwork that the great majority of the men and women who work already bring to their job because of the basic traditions of American life."

THE KEYS TO THE PEOPLE SIDE OF QUALITY

Tom Peters, in addition to being a huge proponent for excellence and innovation, has been a very good collector of information about best practices. Two of his best tips for successful quality management are:

» "Getting everyone on teams is imperative. I'm sick and tired of 50,000-person companies bragging, in their annual reports, about their 125 quality teams. Take the number of people in the firm, divide by ten – if that's not close to your number of teams, you've got a problem.
» Putting teams, especially from disparate functions, together in one location is remarkably powerful. Hanging out together, or even having a private team locker and training area, quickly builds up friendship and understanding – and a willingness to try new approaches and disregard functional barriers."

(Making It Happen, Tom Peters, Journal for Quality and Participation, *March, 1989)*

Improving a task

The best illustration of what a team can do for an organization and what the role of expert is in the system can be found in a team of machine operators for Shick, then a division of Warner-Lambert. The eight machine operators cut razor blades from continuous "ribbons" of blades. Each day they would produce thousands of individual blades ready for packaging in the next step of the process. None of the recent Portuguese immigrants or Italian-American members of the work group had more than a sixth grade education.

When they formed a quality improvement circle, they asked if they could work on making their work easier if it improved production. They met several times and then reported to their supervisor that changing the cutting knife several times a day took too much time and reduced their productivity. They showed that their fastest operator took eight minutes to change the blade that had become dull. "Eight minutes, twice a day for each of us adds up to about 50,000 blades we can't cut in a month," they said. "If someone could help us design it as a single unit that could be pulled out and replaced like a clip in a hunting rifle, we could cut more blades and our work would be easier." An engineer was assigned, and a modular unit was designed (its cost was less in comparison to the increased revenue from the increase in production). The new process of changing a dulled cutting knife took eight seconds. The team knew where savings and their work could be improved; their managers and the people who designed the machines did not because they did not do the work – day after day.

Improving a process

In the early 1990s, a report in the *Cincinnati Enquirer* newspaper reported that John Pepper, then CEO of Procter and Gamble, was very satisfied with the improvements made by teams drawn from across many areas to a significant set of improvements to an entire process at P&G. The next week, many companies in Cincinnati discovered process improvement teams. The companies that dropped them shortly there-after were the ones that limited team membership to managers or "experts." Fred and Merrelyn Emery pioneered the search conference method of strategic planning and improvement. At its heart was their documented research, which, time after time, demonstrated that when groups of people representing those with significant working knowledge of the system in question worked together as "peers," their results consistently outperformed groups "led" by technical experts. In short, those strategic planning groups did what the Shick machine operators did: they identified the problem, formulated a good solution, and then asked experts in to help them design the solution. Popular "quality" programs such as "Six Sigma" are significantly reduced in their effectiveness when they ignore what the machine operators knew, what John Pepper knows, and what the Emerys demonstrated over and over again.

ISO 9000 and employee participation

Amy Zuckerman (co-author) has found, as have many practitioners in the field, that companies get the most value out of their ISO 9000 process when it involves people talking with those who do the work, rather than a team of ISO experts locked away in a room "writing up the quality process and measures that everyone else should, according to their belief, be using." ISO 9000 gives us the shape and structure for a quality management system; it is teams of involved people who make it work for the company.

Pulling the people part all together

In a 1992 article, Phil Crosby laid out what can be called a high-level look at what an executive or a company ought to do to be successful, or 'complete' as he put it, in the twenty-first century (Getting from Here to There, 21st Century Leadership, Philip B. Crosby, *The Journal for Quality and Participation*, July/Aug., 1992). His principles of completeness are as straightforward as his definition of quality.

The principles of completeness are:

» make employees successful;
» make suppliers successful;
» make customers successful.

Crosby says, "Employees will be hard to find, particularly knowledge workers. Machines and processes are becoming so complex, and things change so rapidly, that employees will become the most valuable part of an organization.

Companies will have to search out and nourish them. They will have to:

» Create a climate of consideration in dealing with employees;
» Conduct relentless training;
» Provide education;
» Help people have lives as well as careers.''

Crosby says, customers "will want the product or service to be correct in every respect from the beginning, and more importantly, they will routinely expect that from their suppliers.'' Do that and your customers will be successful.

"Successful suppliers,'' Crosby notes, "will need to have a relationship that permits them to become part of the operation. Companies in all types of business will try to create as little on their own as possible. This means that suppliers will have to be brought into the bowels of the company. They will need to have input concerning future developments, if they are going to meet the financial and productivity requirements.''

KEY PEOPLE IN ISO 9000

The important work done by those involved in developing the ISO 9000 standard was in systematizing the elements necessary for a "quality'' quality management system in any culture or organization while leaving sufficient room within the standard for specific applications of quality methods. In practice, however, a number of sectors felt the need for standards covering issues common to their sector but not to others. Such industry-specific need has been met by the development of industry-specific standards such as TL 9000 and AS 9000.

Because the ISO management system is a "living'' or evolutionary process, the many players worldwide who have had or still have an impact on the development and maintenance of the ISO 9000 standard are as important to the world of quality management as are its key thinkers or theorists. Even though there are far too many to list here, we will note the key players. It should be noted first, however, that primary input on ISO 9000 came from the Canadian Standards

Association (CSA), which has served as secretariat (or administrator) of ISO Technical Committee (TC) 176 for quality management and quality assurance – the originator and ongoing maintenance forum for the standard. CSA staff members with key influence, both current and retired, include Peter Ford, Kevin McKinley, and Grant Gillis who is current secretary of TC 176.

Since 1997, Pierre Caillibot has chaired TC 176. Over the years he also served as Chair of the Canadian National Committee for ISO and has chaired, or otherwise been involved in, a number of Canadian and international technical committees, work groups and task groups dealing with a variety of quality-related issues.

Others who carried on this work and helped refocus the original standard include another Canadian, Gary Hilton, who headed up the Canadian delegation for ISO TC 176, and has been a member of Working Group (WG) 18 of subcommittee 22 within TC 176, which is currently working on the next revision of ISO 9000.

In the United States both Jeff Hooper and Jack West have been instrumental in promoting ISO 9000 revisions. Mr Hooper, who's employed at Lucent Technologies, is credited with spearheading the ISO 9000:2000 revisions. Jack West was a key player within ISO/TC 176 in developing the eight quality management principles of ISO 9000. West is now the Chair of the US TAG to ISO TC 176 and lead delegate for the United States to the International Standards Organization committee responsible for the ISO 9000 family of quality management standards. He is also a member of the board of directors of the Registrar Accreditation Board (RAB). In addition, Bob Marshall was co-convener of the ISO Working Group (WG) that developed ISO 9000–3:1997, the guidance standard for applying ISO 9001 to the software industry. Since 1997, he has been a member of ISO/TC176/WC2/WG18, which developed the year 2000 revisions of ISO 9001 and ISO 9004, responsible for developing Information Technology (IT) tools to aid development of the standards work.

Based in France, Youssef El Gammal has served as chairman of ISO TC 176 subcommittee 1, whose focus is the ISO 9000 standards series. And in England, William Truscott has worked hard on ISO 9000 fundamentals and vocabulary as convener of TC 176 subcommittee

1/working group 1. As convener of TC 69, subcommittee 1/working group 2, he is responsible for the development of ISO 3534-02 for Statistics, Vocabulary and Symbols, which combined breaking new ground and acting as the basis for communication and understanding of quality management issues.

Quality and Quality Management Resources

» Associations, institutes, and centers
  » ISO-related resources
» World Wide Web sites
» Recommended books
» Recommended articles

[Author's note: This is not a definitive listing of associations, articles, books or Websites devoted to, or with a significant interest in, quality and quality management. It is a listing of organizations that we know of that offer a great deal of theory and practice-based content and an opportunity to network with experienced practitioners. That is not to say that those not listed are any less knowledgdable; only that we are not familiar enough with them to list them, nor is there sufficient room here.]

ASSOCIATIONS, INSTITUTES, AND CENTERS

The American National Standards Institute

The American National Standards Institute's mission is to enhance both the global competitiveness of US business and the US quality of life by promoting and facilitating voluntary consensus standards and conformity assessment systems, and safeguarding their integrity. http://www.ansi.org/

The Asian Productivity Organization

http://www.apo-tokyo.org/

The Asian Productivity Organization was created in 1961 to oversee productivity development throughout Asia and the Pacific. Today, the APO serves as the umbrella organization for 18 countries to coordinate and assist their individual productivity activities.

The Association for Quality and Participation

The Association for Quality and Participation (AQP) is an international not-for-profit membership association dedicated to improving work-places through quality and participation practices. In 2001, it affiliated with the ASQ. http://www.aqp.org

Publications:

» The AQP has sponsored a Team Excellence Award since 1985.
» *The Journal for Quality and Participation* is the official journal for the AQP and is a leading journal in its field.
» "News For A Change" is the newsletter of the AQP.

The Australian Quality Council

The Australian Quality Council's role is to assist organizations in achieving world-class performance using the Australian Business Excellence Framework. http://www.aqc.org.au/index.html

The American Society for Quality

The American Society for Quality (ASQ) has been the leading quality improvement organization in the United States for more than 50 years. http://www.asq.org/
Publications:

» *Quality Progress* – ASQ's flagship publication includes in-depth articles describing the application of innovative methods in areas such as knowledge management, process improvement, and organizational behavior.
» *Six Sigma Forum Magazine* – ASQ's newest publication. The first magazine to address the various developmental needs of Six Sigma professionals.

Australian National University

Online introduction to Statistical Control Charts at the Australian National University
http://www.anu.edu.au/nceph/surfstat/surfstat-home/cont5.html

Best Manufacturing Practices

Best Manufacturing Practices (BMP) website: http://www.bmpcoe.org/
The BMP Center of Excellence is a partnership among the Office of Naval Research's BMP Program, the Department of Commerce's Bureau of Export Administration, and the University of Maryland's Engineering Research Center.
Three superior databases are available for free downloading. http://www.bmpcoe.org/pmws/index.html

British Standards Institute

The British Standards Institute (BSI) provides expertise in product testing, CE marking, global trade inspection, environmental management, information security, and provision of technical advice to exporters. http://www.bsi-global.com/index.html

BSI's *Business Standards Magazine* is an online publication that covers all aspects of standards development and applications through news reports, interviews, and case studies. http://www.bsiamericas.com/bsi_site/bizstand/index.html

W. Edwards Deming Institute

The aim of the Institute is to foster understanding of *The Deming System of Profound Knowledge*™ to advance commerce, prosperity, and peace. http://www.deming.org/

European Forum for Teamwork

Established in 1982 and now with more than 300 member organizations, the European Forum for Teamwork is the UK's leading authority on improving performance through increasing employee involvement and teamwork.
http://www.efteam.org/

European Foundation for Quality Management

The European Foundation for Quality Management (EFQM) was founded in 1988 by the Presidents of 14 major European companies, with the endorsement of the European Commission. http://www.efqm.org/

The European Quality Prizes are presented to organizations that demonstrate excellence in the management of quality as their fundamental process for continuous improvement.

European Organization for Quality

The European Organization for Quality (EOQ) is the European interdisciplinary organization striving for effective improvement in the sphere of quality management. Established in 1956, the EOQ's present membership is 34 national European quality organizations. http://www.eoq.org/

European Quality is the official Journal of the EOQ and is a high-level management publication focused on Quality in all aspects. http://www.eoq.org/WhatIsEOQ_EuropeanQualityJournal.html

Inventing the Organization of the 21st Century

Home for MIT's Inventing the Organization of the 21st Century: http://ccs.mit.edu/21c/

Thomas Malone, along with Peter Senge and Thomas Kochan, are co-founders. An interesting and informative white paper or manifesto in PDF format is available. Center for Coordination Science.

Motorola University

One of the original quality universities, Motorola has been a quality leader since winning the Baldrige Award in 1988. Twenty years ago, Motorola University began. Today, it is widely recognized as a premier Corporate University. http://mu.motorola.com/

Motorola University has been integral in advancing critical Motorola business initiatives like Six Sigma Quality, Total Cycle Time Reduction, and System Availability.

National Institute of Standards and Technology

National Institute of Standards and Technology (NIST): http://www.nist.gov

NIST's mission is to develop and promote measurement, standards, and technology to enhance productivity, facilitate trade, and improve the quality of life. NIST programs that relate to quality management include:

» A nationwide Manufacturing Extension Partnership with a network of local centers offering technical and business assistance to smaller manufacturers; http://www.mep.nist.gov/

» Malcolm Baldrige National Quality Award is the centerpiece of the Baldrige National Quality Program. This award, which since 1988 has been presented annually by the President to recognize performance excellence, focuses on an organization's overall performance management system; http://www.quality.nist.gov/

» Quality software available from the US National Institute of Standards and Technology; http://www.nist.gov/public_affairs/software.htm

» Conformance Test Suite Software;
» Dataplot;
» Design of Experiments.

Quality Function Deployment Institute

Quality Function Deployment Institute (QFD) – In 1996, Dr Yoji Akao, co-founder of QFD, convinced that the substantial evolution and contribution of QFD worldwide merited recognition of those who had made it possible, agreed to the creation of a Prize in his honor. http://www.qfdi.org/

Quality Network

The Quality Network in the UK is still a great source for information on quality management and ISO 9000. http://www.quality.co.uk/

Quality Society of Australasia

The Quality Society of Australasia (QSA) offers Fellow and Member grades to quality practitioners and people from other disciplines using quality principles and practices in their work. http://www.qsanet.com/
   Publications:

» *Momentum*, the quality magazine, published quarterly, is complimentary to members of the Society.
» Hot Qews, the e-newsletter delivered to your inbox 6 times per year to keep you up to date on QSA's activities, networking events and current issues.
» QSA Edge – the new information service bulletin containing summaries of key articles from international management literature.

Shingo Prize for Excellence in Manufacturing

The Shingo Prize for Excellence in Manufacturing was established in 1988 in honor of Shigeo Shingo. http://www.shingoprize.org/shingo/index.html
   The Prize promotes world-class manufacturing and recognizes companies that achieve superior customer satisfaction and business results.

The philosophy of the Shingo Prize is that world-class business performance may be achieved through focused improvements in core manufacturing and business processes.

South African Quality Institute

The South African Quality Institute (SAQI) is the umbrella body that coordinates the Quality effort in South Africa.
http://www.saqi.co.za/Enter.htm
   Publications:

» *Management Today*, which contains SAQI's quality awareness and information supplement.
» *The Quality Edge* also provides excellent advertising opportunities.
» *The SAQI Update*, a monthly newsletter.

ISO 9000-RELATED RESOURCES

British Standards Institute

The British Standards Institute (BSI) provides expertise in product testing, CE marking, global trade inspection, environmental management, information security, and provision of technical advice to exporters. http://www.bsi-global.com/index.html

BSI's *Business Standards Magazine* is an online publication that covers all aspects of standards development and applications through news reports, interviews, and case studies. http://www.bsiamericas.com/bsi_site/bizstand/index.html

Det Norske Veritas (DNV)

Over the past 10 years, DNV has issued 28,837 ISO 9000-series certificates in over 40 countries and 2,182 ISO 14000 certificates. http://www.dnv.com/

ISO

International Organization for Standardization – http://www.iso.ch/iso/en/ISOOnline.frontpage

Based in Geneva, Switzerland, ISO is a non-governmental organization established in 1947 that promotes the development of standardization and related activities. Its newsletters can be a good source of information on updates on ISO matters. Annual reports and figures on how many organizations are adopting/being accredited various standards.

General information on the ISO 9000 standards can be found at ISO's Technical Committee no. 176, Sub-committee no. 2 (ISO/TC 176/SC 2): http://isotc176sc2.elysium-ltd.net/.

ISO Bulletin provides a monthly overview of ISO's activities. For information on how to best meet ISO 9000 requirements in the USA, contact the American Society of Quality (ASQ) in Milwaukee, Wisc. ASQ maintains an information line on ISO 9000 and other quality issues. The toll-free number is: 800–952–6587.

WORLD WIDE WEB SITES

Concurrent Engineering Toolkit

The Concurrent Engineering Toolkit (CE-Toolkit) is an Internet agent that enables the rapid identification, evaluation, installation, and integration of the resources required to implement agile manufacturing networks. http://ce-toolkit.crd.ge.com/ce-toolkit/homepage.html

MCB University Press

MCB University Press, in addition to being a publisher of leading quality management journals, is also a portal to abstracts of the world's 400 leading business journals. Highly recommended. http://www.mcb.co.uk/

Bill Casti

Bill Casti may well be one of the most helpful quality management fanatics, in the best sense of the word. His Website takes a bit of navigating, but everything on quality management is there someplace. http://www.quality.org/

TheRiteStuff

TheRiteStuff is a new Website designed and operated by Patricia McLagan of Washington, DC, and Durban, South Africa, a leading researcher and practitioner in helping organizations transform themselves for modern operations; http://www.theritestuff.com/main.asp. The site connects businesspeople with best practices that have been documented to produce positive business results.

Links to Statistical Software Providers
http://www.stata.com/support/links/stat_software.html

RECOMMENDED BOOKS

[Author's tips/notes: Books that are "out of print" are now available through resale on the Internet. Amazon.com, for example, both solicits and lists used books that individuals wish to sell. Many of the Internet book sales sites also supply access to customer's own "recommended books" for quality, quality management, etc.]

Amsden, Robert T., Howard E. Butler and Davida M. Amsden
SPC Simplified
Practical Steps to Quality
Paperback – 304-pages ©1998
The simplest, best approach to introducing everyone to this most basic tool of quality.

Asaka, Tetsuichi and Kazuo Ozeki
Handbook of Quality Tools
The Japanese Approach
Paperback – 315-pages ©1996
A comprehensive training aid as well as hands-on reference book for supervisors, team leaders, and foremen.

Brown, Mark Graham
Baldrige Award Winning Quality 11th Edition
How to Interpret the Baldrige Criteria for Performance Excellence
(Baldridge Award Winning Quality, 11th edn)
Paperback – 417-pages ©2001
The definitive reference for interpreting the Baldrige Criteria.

Crosby, Philip B.
Completeness, Quality for the 21st Century
Dutton 1992
250–pages
ISBN: 0-525-93475-8
Perhaps one of the best books for senior executives. A look at the future of success from a very high level.

Deming, W. Edwards
The New Economics: For Industry, Government, Education
247–pages 1st edition (January 15, 2000)
MIT Press; ISBN: 0262541165

Feigenbaum, Armand V.
Total Quality Control, Revised (Fortieth Anniversary Edition)
Hardcover – 896–pages 3rd edition (1991)
McGraw-Hill Professional Publishing; ISBN: 0070203547
The beginning of total quality control and still one of the best sources for those interested in what was termed TQM a few years ago.

Hamson, Ned, Frank Heckman, Tom Lyons, Kaat Exterbille, Peter Beerten
After Atlantis: Working, Managing, and Leading in Turbulent Times
Paperback – 192–pages (October 1997) Butterworth-Heinemann (Trd); ISBN: 0750698845

Guide to Quality Control
ASIN: 9283310357
This book shows supervisors and line personnel how to apply the on-line quality control techniques that revolutionized Japanese manufacturing and are now revitalizing industry in other parts of the world.

Ishikawa, Kaoru, Editor
QC Circle Activities
Organizational Quality and Customer Satisfaction
Quality Circles
Management Presentations
Union of Japanese Scientists and Engineers
1958

Juran, Joseph M.
Juran on Leadership for Quality: An Executive Handbook
Hardcover – 376–pages (February 1989)
Free Press; ISBN: 0029166829

Kano, Noriaki, Editor
Guide To TQM In Service Industries
260–pages, 1996, APO
ISBN: 92-833-1130-2 (Paper) $20.00
Guide to TQM in Japanese service companies, including a hotel, utility, retail store chain, and bank, as well as the Deming Prize-winning Florida & Light. Discusses the future of service industries and the role of TQM.

Mizuno, Shigeru
Management for Quality Improvement
The 7 New QC Tools

Mizuno, Shigeru and Yoji Akao, Editors
QFD: The Customer Driven Approach to Quality Planning and Deployment
APO, 365–pages, 1993
ISBN: 92-833-1122-1 (Paper) $22.00
This book details quality function deployment activities, provides insights into the use of the quality chart for tracking characteristics, introduces simultaneous multi-dimension design for high efficiency production, outlines how to eliminate causes of failure through pre-production corrective measures, and discusses process design and quality deployment.

Osada, Takashi
The 5S's: Five Keys to a Total Quality Environment
APO, 211–pages, 1991 (9th printing 2000)
ISBN: 92-833-1116-7 (Paper) $12.00
Takashi Osada explores the basic philosophy behind the 5S campaign, and explains how every workplace can benefit from its use.

Peach, Robert W., Bill Peach, Diane S. Ritter
The Memory Jogger 9000/2000: A Pocket Guide to Implementing the ISO 9001 Quality Systems Standard Based on Bsr/Iso/Asq

Q9001-2000
Paperback (November 2000)
Goal/QPC; ISBN: 1576810321

Peters, Tom
Thriving on Chaos: Handbook for a Management Revolution
Harper & Row, New York, NY, 1988
708-pages
ISBN: 0-06-097184-3

Revelle, Jack B.
Manufacturing Handbook of Best Practices: An Innovation, Productivity, and Quality Focus
Hardcover (October 2001)
Saint Lucie Press; ISBN: 1574443003

Senge, Peter M.
The Fifth Discipline: The Art and Practice of the Learning Organization
Paperback - 423-pages (October 1994)
Currency/Doubleday; ISBN: 0385260954

Shingo, Shigeo, Andrew P. Dillon (Translator), Shingo Shigeo
The Shingo Production Management System: Improving Process Functions
Hardcover - 238-pages (March 1992)
Productivity Pr; ISBN: 0915299526

Taguchi, Genichi, Subir Chowdhury, Yuin Wu
The Mahalanobis - Taguchi System
Hardcover - 300-pages 1st edition (August 29, 2000)
McGraw-Hill Professional Publishing; ISBN: 0071362630

Townsend, Patrick L. and Joan E. Gebhardt
Commit to Quality
Paperback - 208-pages 1 edition (March 23, 1990)
John Wiley & Sons; ISBN: 0471520187

Zuckerman, Amy
ISO 9000 Made Easy: A Cost-Saving Guide to Documentation and

Registration
ASIN: 0814402526

RECOMMENDED ARTICLES

[Authors' note: While there are literally thousands of articles available, the ones selected here are those you would want to have stored away just in case your server crashed for good or your library burned to the ground.]

Quality management and leadership

Brown, Mark Graham
Defining Customer Requirements Service Quality Deployment
The Journal for Quality and Participation, March 1990
Quality function deployment (QFD) as applied to a service sector example.

Cabana, Steven and Janet Fiero
The Motorola Mini-Chip operation's search for its future . . . Motorola, strategic planning and the search conference
The Journal for Quality and Participation, July/August 1995
An excellent case study of how the search conference can be used for strategic planning of quality management

Crosby, Philip B.
Getting from Here to There, 21st Century Leadership
The Journal for Quality and Participation, July/Aug. 1992
The essence of his book on completeness. Leadership in quality from the senior executive's view.

Deming, W. Edwards
The Need for Change: Quality and the Required Style of Management
The Journal for Quality and Participation, March 1988
In this concise article, Deming lays out the core of how to manage for quality results.

Feigenbaum, Armand V., Dr
Seven Keys to Constant Quality: Quality Pushes vs. Quality Foundations
The Journal for Quality and Participation, March 1989

Feigenbaum, Armand V., Dr
Designing for America's Quality Future with Quality Leadership . . .
Managing for Tomorrow's Competitiveness Today
The Journal for Quality and Participation, March 1996

Ishikawa, Kaoru, Dr
Group Wide Quality Control: Necessary Conditions for Success and
Survival
The Journal for Quality and Participation, March 1998
In this last article written before his death, for an American audience, Dr
Ishikawa lays out his broad vision of quality's impact on the enterprise,
employees and the larger community.

Juran, J.M.
From Shoddiness to World Leadership The Evolution of Japanese Lead-
ership Quality
The Journal for Quality and Participation, July/Aug 1991

Lyons, Tom
This Large Scale Process Works Well in Single or Multi-Site Organiza-
tions and in Communities . . . Shared Learning: A Proven Participative
Change Design
The Journal for Quality & Participation, March 1996

Peters, Tom
Making It Happen: Coming to Grips with the Dismal Record of Quality
Program Implementation
The Journal for Quality and Participation, March 1989

Peters, Tom
Total Quality Leadership Let's Get It Right
The Journal for Quality and Participation, March 1991

Senge, Peter
The Real Message of the Quality Movement Building Learning Organi-
zations
The Journal for Quality and Participation, March 1992
Senge synthesizes the teachings of Deming with the innovative scenario
planning approach of Arie de Geus

Petersen, Donald E., CEO of Ford Motor Company
The Basic Tools of Global Competition: Can America Compete?
The Journal for Quality and Participation, June 1988

Smith, Frederick W., CEO of Federal Express
Excellence in People, Service, and Profits Requires Creating an Empowering Environment for All Employees
The Journal for Quality and Participation, June 1990

Smith, Roger B. CEO of General Motors
Revving Up a Mature Giant
The Journal for Quality and Participation, June 1989

ISO 9000

Allaire, Paul A., CEO of Xerox
Training 100,000 is Just the Beginning in the Race Without a Finish Line Quality Improvement: A Never Ending Journey
The Journal for Quality and Participation, March 1990

Allaire, Paul A., CEO of Xerox
Two Years After the Baldrige Quality and Beyond
The Journal for Quality and Participation, March 1992

Allaire, Paul A., CEO of Xerox
The Xerox Method of Duplicating Success
The Journal for Quality and Participation, Jan/Feb 1998, Vol. 21, No. 1
ISO 9000

Beardsley, Jeff – JBH Assoc., Dick Schaefer – Kind & Knox Gelatine, Inc.
Bits of truth; lots of rumors, myths, fears and downright ignorance; what's it really like? One company's journey to ISO 9000 registration
The Journal for Quality and Participation, March 1995

Buell, Hal and Amy Zuckerman
Information, Please
The Journal for Quality & Participation, May/June 1999, Vol. 22, No 3

ISO 9000 is at base not just a documentation system, it can be a vital part of a knowledge-building communication system.

Gasko, Helen M.
Here's How One Company Did It in Four Months
You Can Earn ISO 9002 Approval in Less Than a Year
The Journal for Quality and Participation, March 1992

Reimann, Curt and Harry S. Hertz
Can't We Just Do ISO 9000? What's the Difference Between it and the Baldrige? The Baldrige Award and ISO 9000 Registration Compared
The Journal for Quality & Participation, Jan/Feb 1996
Curt Reimann was the director of the Baldrige Award from its inception until 1997. Harry Hurtz became the director after Reimann's retirement.

Zuckerman, Amy
You're getting into the ISO 9000 certification process? A guide to selecting your ISO 9000 consultant
The Journal for Quality and Participation, Oct/Nov 1993

Zuckerman, Amy
Did You Expect More Out of Your ISO 9000 Process? Adding Value to Your ISO 9000 Process
The Journal for Quality and Participation, Jan/Feb 1996

Ten Steps to Making it Work

- » The "one best way" myth
  - » The Baldrige, ISO 9000, and the EFQM model compared
- » Jump starting your quality management system
- » Measured approaches to implementing a quality management system
  - » Ten steps to total quality
  - » ISO's suggested steps for beginning a quality management system
  - » Ten steps to make ISO 9000 work for you
  - » Seven ways to launch a *Value – Added ISO 9000*™ process

PULLING IT ALL TOGETHER

[Authors' note: If your organization already had a quality management system and you are looking into getting an ISO 9000 audit and registration, then you should, perhaps, skip down to the boxes that contain suggested steps for that process.]

The "one best way" myth

There is not and cannot be any single set of 10 ways to implement a quality management system. The reason is based upon one of the basic tenets of quality management, namely that there is "no one best way" to do anything. The reason is simple: the system is in constant change.

» When customer's requirements change, the methods to meet them must be adapted to the new requirements.
» As technology changes, the technology used in any task will change.
» People are not all alike!

The idea that people are not all alike may seem obvious but in most organizations today, you will still see workstations, machines, computers, etc. all selected and designed to meet a range of heights, weights, and physical capabilities determined by purchasing and the manufacturers of the products and not by the people who must then "fit" themselves to the workstation, machine or computer, etc.

The first of Dr Deming's Five Principles also tells why there can be no one best way: "The central problem in lack of quality is the failure of management to understand variation. (Everything varies. Statistics help us to predict how much it is going to vary.)"

That said, we can, however, recommend the logical first two steps that apply as they would to almost any management or organizational initiative:

Step 1

Ask yourself three questions:

1 Is creating a quality management system for your organization something you feel, or know, that you "have" to do?

Examples: *If you cannot reduce the number of returns, and lost customers, you'll be out of business in three years. You know you will lose one or more major customers if you are not ISO 9000 registered within a specified time.*

If you answer yes, go to the next question.

Some different ways of asking question one that help you get the information you need and either input on areas that you may have overlooked, or confirmation that you are on the right track:

2 What do you hope to accomplish, or gain, by creating a quality management system for your organization?

Write down your answer.

Is it measurable? In other words, will you be able to tell when and/or if you have achieved your initial goal(s)?

Don't start until you can set some initial measurable goal or goals.

3 Are you willing to be personally involved in the planning, design, and implementation of the quality management system?

If the answer is no or a qualified yes, don't start. Go back to the first two questions and take more time to think about the implications of saying no to number one, or not having measurable goals for number two.

Step 2

Learn as much about purpose(s) of quality improvement and different quality management systems as possible and how they match up with your overall goals and the processes your organization uses to deliver its product(s) and/or service(s) to your customers BEFORE enlisting anyone else to assist in the organizational search and learning process.

» Take a hard look at what the leading lights have to say about what quality management is and is not, and what it requires from an organization's leader, managers, and employees. Does one or several of these leading thinkers seem to "fit" the needs of your organization? Select one or more approaches for further investigation.

A colleague who was responsible for designing and giving quality and team training to thousands of managers and union workers at

General Motors in the early 1980s and monitoring the Saturn process in the late 1990s says that one way to decide which approach to use – Deming, Crosby, or Juran – is to use all three. "Use Crosby's approach to train the frontline workers, supervisors, managers, and marketing; use Juran's methods and approach for design and engineering, safety, and the quality department; and be sure that the folks at the executive level understand and can apply Dr Deming's management philosophy."

» Find some peers or organizations that have used the approach(es) you are looking into and ask them about their experiences and assessments from when they began to the present.

» Select which quality model you are gong to use as your macro-guide. If you look at the Baldrige, ISO 9000:2000, and the EFQM Model, you will see that there is substantial agreement on the "parts" or categories that make up quality management. How they are put together specifically should be driven by the needs of your firm and its present and future customers.

Author's tip: *How can I keep track of all the information that we gather on quality management? There is so much information out there!* A good way, perhaps, to think about the three "models" is that whichever one you work from will serve as your mental "filing system" for further information you gather along the way. Of course, you might end up cross-filing a number of items but you will have reduced the number of choices of how to store and retrieve the information to 7–9.

Table 10.1 compares the Baldrige, ISO 9000, and EFQM models.

At this point, you have several choices in how to use the remainder of this chapter:

1 If you have to become ISO 9000:2000 registered, you might want to skip down to the ISO 9000:2000 section. There you will find ISO suggestions on the steps involved in establishing a quality management system, and two sets of steps suggested by Amy Zuckerman as to how to approach ISO 9000 registration, as well as to how to get the most value out of your ISO 9000:2000 system.

Table 10.1 The Baldridge, ISO 9000, and EFQM model compared.

2001 Malcolm Baldridge National Quality Award Categories	ISO 9000:2000: Its eight quality management principles	The EFQM Model
1 Leadership 120	Principle 1 Customer focus	1 Leadership
2 Strategic planning 85	Principle 2 Leadership	2 People
3 Customer and market focus 85	Principle 3 Involvement of people	3 People results
4 Information and analysis 90	Principle 4 Process approach	4 Key performance results
5 Human resource focus 85	Principle 5 System approach to management	5 Policy and strategy
6 Process management 85	Principle 6 Continual improvement	6 Processes
7 Business results 450	Principle 7 Factual approach to decision making	7 Customer results
(Items' point values indicate relative importance)	Principle 8 Mutually beneficial supplier relationships	8 Society results
	Principle 9 Partnerships and resources	

2 If you are beginning a quality management system as part of your long-range plan and you do not have a pressing quality problem to address, then you might want to move to the "Ten steps to total quality" or the suggested steps by ISO.

  Note: If your organization is in manufacturing, distribution, and/or transport, we strongly suggest that you add Dr Ishikawa's, G. Taguchi's, and Shigeo Shingo's books (listed in the Resources chapter) to your study of Crosby, Deming, and Juran.

3 If you have determined that you need to make significant progress in particular areas, then you might want to consider some ways to jump start your quality management process, as is discussed below.

JUMP STARTING YOUR QUALITY MANAGEMENT SYSTEM

''There's not much time left for us,'' said the plant manager of a parts manufacturer. ''In the automotive industry today, if we can't deliver quality, we might as well give up.'' He was very frustrated because his plant in Monck's Corner, South Carolina, had serious quality problems, even though for many months he had been doing all of the things that were supposed to produce improvement.

He had made quality his personal concern; he had invested in training programs; he had encouraged initiative-taking at the lower levels; and, at considerable expense, he had inaugurated a program of supervisor/employee quality committees that met regularly and developed hundreds of ideas for improvement. What to do? Some of his associates urged that the programs be continued and strengthened.

The plant manager selected the production line that was having the most costly problems and asked its manager to reduce the most prevalent defect on that line by some significant amount, and to do it quickly. The manager gathered a team of employees, supervisors, and engineers and, together, they planned a series of steps to reduce full slab cure defects. They achieved their first improvement goal within the next few weeks. With that accomplished, they extended their effort. Improvement was under way. Within months, the entire plant's performance had measurably improved.

A series of successful focused projects provides data on what the organization can accomplish if it stretches; which is vital input for shaping a corporate quality strategy rooted in reality. Without direct linkages to tangible achievements, corporate quality strategies remain pious hopes, slogans, and platitudes.

The critical ingredients that cause people to step up to the job in a fresh way, to experiment, to feel empowered, to make it happen, are the following.

1 There is an urgent and compelling goal that must be achieved.
2 The goal is clear and measurable and success can be experienced quickly.
3 There is a realization that the monkey is on your back and you can't escape accountability.

4 You understand that you must do whatever is needed to reach the goal, even if it is a bit unconventional.[1]

People may wonder whether this is merely another example of the traditional quick fix that spurts, then sputters and disappears. After you have selected a high-profile problem and selected the group to work on it, you also require that they use the elements (appropriate to the specific problem) that are so essential to supporting and sustaining what will become your organization's ongoing quality effort, such as: statistical quality control; quality diagnostics and troubleshooting; customer needs assessments; training; employee involvement; improved measurement; and so forth.

We might consider this to be the "Nike/Toyota" method. Nike is known for its slogan, "Just Do It!" Just Do It! aptly describes the bias of people in operations – they are geared for action, not planning. The traditional ways to launch quality management throughout an organization leave many in operations to chafe at the bit and even resist the quality effort. Schaffer's "Quality, Now!" approach has the advantage of not fighting but cooperating with the bias of operations. Toyota is really quite good at planning and we could characterize their superior quality management and manufacturing process in the phrase, "Let's Plan It!" It is no coincidence that the "Let's Plan It!" approach is the preferred approach of those with accounting, legal, and engineering backgrounds. Their bias is for planning before doing.

If we look at Schaffer's approach with Toyota's lenses, we can see that asking the following two questions of managers and others in the organization will help you find areas where "Just Do It!" and "Let's Plan It!" work together, rather than oppose each other.

» What problem or what process needs improvement right now to keep our heads above water in the coming year?
» What opportunity do you see that we'd be absolute fools not to try to take advantage of in the coming year?

And if you select that approach to create the setting for a strategic breakthrough for your organization, it will concretely demonstrate the value of using quality tools to achieve breakthroughs for yourselves and the firm. Your next step? You will have created the momentum for launching a company-wide approach, so one of the ten or more step processes will now be more effective. And in a crunch, people know they have new reliable tools to look to.

MEASURED APPROACHES TO IMPLEMENTING A QUALITY MANAGEMENT SYSTEM

TEN STEPS TO TOTAL QUALITY

1 Create an awareness of quality and the philosophy of constant improvement – Total quality, particularly in a service business, is employee involvement since what's for sale is not merely product, but the attitudes, values, and behaviors of employees who deliver that product and service. This can be done in quality awareness training sessions in which groups of employees are challenged to think up better ways of doing routine things like filling orders, handling complaints, providing information, dealing with the transfer of paperwork, and unblocking interdepartmental dead-ends. Management can draw immediate ideas from these sessions and take action at once. Employees will see their ideas in action and will be likely to buy into participating in teams on a longer-term basis.

2 Have all employees identify their top priority jobs – Seldom do employees view their top priority job in terms of meeting and exceeding customer needs. Too often, they see it as satisfying the boss or transacting some technical or in-house operation. Employees must be taught that everyone in a service company is involved in serving the external company. To understand this, they must see how their actions impact subsequent operations that inevitably reach out to the end user. This realization will eventually result in a team approach to dealing with customers.

3 Make your organization's vision a personal mission for every employee – Too many organizations have vision and mission statements that are full of high-sounding phrases that mean

little to a data entry clerk who, in completing customer bills, is the closest interface to the customer. While a vision statement about quality and excellent service is important, a process for making that vision come alive must be apparent to every employee.

4 Examine organizational values and systems that might be a barrier to quality – before adopting a total quality customer focus, service organizations must do a little self-analysis and remove reward systems and contradictory practices that will make it nearly impossible for employees to take quality seriously. One retailer, for instance, adopted a three-in-line policy, which said they would not allow customer lines to exceed three people. At the same time, they insisted employees finish stocking shelves and never leave half-empty supply carts in aisles. Since their department managers were concerned with well-stocked shelves, the choice was simple, and the customer was left waiting until the store manager charged out of his office to round up check-out people to deal with long lines.

5 Empower employees to act – Service organizations should work like one quality manufacturer who, when the "blue light" goes on the front office, empties until the shop-floor problem that it signals is handled.

6 Survey customers personally – In any organization that deals directly with customers, first-line service people represent a vital marketing tool that is seldom tapped. To make the most of this invaluable feedback, service companies must train their first-line people to constantly seek and interpret feedback on all the perceptions of service their customers hold. Next, they must be provided with open channels of communication to feed this information back through the organization until it reaches those who can take immediate action on it. Of course, no organization can adopt a truly open and listening attitude if they are unwilling or unable to hear bad news from other departments.

7 Identify next process customers as team members – When an organization begins to treat employees like customers they

begin to identify their survival with customer satisfaction and with the satisfaction of co-workers. This sets the stage for a powerfully reinforced team concept in which everyone feels a driving need to work together and share information and feedback.

8 Measure meaningful events, not just what's easy to measure – Achieving a high level of service quality requires creative approaches to setting, measuring, and tracking agreed-upon indicators that reflect important standards rather than the most obvious and easily tabulated events. They can measure such things as customer satisfaction indices, simplified processes, or time savings.

9 Adopt a performance management system that rewards teamwork, constant improvement, and new behaviors consistent with interdepartmental cooperation – Total quality depends on a total overhaul in most performance management systems. The changes needed will impact appraisal forms, the appraisal cycle, and the use of rewards and sanctions. To begin with, when an organization moves toward a total quality structure, roles and responsibilities change. Executives will be asked to take a much more personal approach to working with problem-solving teams, managers will become team leaders, and supervisors will be asked to involve subordinates in everyday decision making, gradually assisting them to take over some traditional supervisory roles.

The performance management system can either drive or restrain these kinds of changes. When the system continues to measure objectives which are not cross-functional or quality related, it will get in the way of efforts to change behavior.

10 Establish an ongoing process of executive involvement – Senior managers must take an active role in getting out and about. They must do the service equivalent of "getting out on the shop floor," meeting employees and customers and holding heart-to-heart talks with them.[2]

ISO'S SUGGESTED STEPS FOR BEGINNING A QUALITY MANAGEMENT SYSTEM

IMPLEMENTING YOUR ISO 9001:2000 QUALITY MANAGEMENT SYSTEM[3]

1. Identify the goals you want to achieve. Typical goals may be:
   - » Be more efficient and profitable.
   - » Produce products and services that consistently meet customer requirements.
   - » Achieve customer satisfaction.
   - » Increase market share.
   - » Maintain market share.
   - » Improve communications and morale in the organization.
   - » Reduce costs and liabilities.
   - » Increase confidence in the production system.
2. Identify what others expect of you. These are the expectations of interested parties (stakeholders) such as:
   - » Customers and end users
   - » Employees
   - » Suppliers
   - » Shareholders
   - » Society.
3. Obtain information about the ISO 9000 family.
   - » For more detailed information, see ISO 9000:2000, ISO 9001:2000 and ISO 9004:2000.
   - » For supporting information, refer to the ISO Website.
   - » For implementation case studies and news of ISO 9000 developments worldwide, read the ISO publication ISO Management Systems.
4. Apply the ISO 9000 family of standards in your management system. Decide if you are seeking certification that your quality management system is in conformance with ISO 9001:2000 or if you are preparing to apply for a national quality award.
   - » Use ISO 9001:2000 as the basis for certification.
   - » Use ISO 9004:2000 in conjunction with your national quality award criteria to prepare for a national quality award.

5 Obtain guidance on specific topics within the quality management system. These topic-specific standards are:
   » ISO 10006 for project management
   » ISO 10007 for configuration management
   » ISO 10012 for measurement systems
   » ISO 10013 for quality documentation
   » ISO/TR 10014 for managing the economics of quality
   » ISO 10015 for training
   » ISO/TS 16949 for automotive suppliers
   » ISO 19011 for auditing.
6 Establish your current status, determine the gaps between your quality management system and the requirements of ISO 9001:2000. You may use one or more of the following:
   » Self-assessment
   » Assessment by an external organization.
7 Determine the processes that are needed to supply products to your customers. Review the requirements of the ISO 9001:2000 section on Product Realization to determine how they apply or do not apply to your quality management system, including:
   » Customer-related processes
   » Design and/or development
   » Purchasing
   » Production and service operations
   » Control of measuring and monitoring devices.
8 Develop a plan to close the gaps in step 6 and to develop the processes in step 7.
   » Identify actions needed to close the gaps, allocate resources to perform these actions, assign responsibilities, and establish a schedule to complete the needed actions. ISO 9001:2000 Paragraphs 4.1 and 7.1 provide the information you will need to consider when developing the plan.
9 Carry out your plan. Proceed to implement the identified actions and track progress to your schedule.
10 Undergo periodic internal assessment. Use ISO 19011 for guidance in auditing, auditor qualification, and managing audit programs.

11 Do you need to demonstrate conformance? If yes, go to step 12.
12 Undergo independent audit. Engage an accredited registration/certification body to perform an audit and certify that your quality management system complies with the requirements of ISO 9001:2000.

TEN STEPS TO MAKE ISO 9000 WORK FOR YOU

How a company proceeds with ISO 9000 registration can make a tremendous difference in terms of cost savings. Many companies have been known to move ahead quickly with ISO 9000 documentation and other processes only to hire a registrar and have previous work rejected. Other companies have hired unaccredited registrars only to have their certificates rejected. These sorts of experiences add up to unnecessary financial losses.

Through interviews with hundreds of companies worldwide, this author has identified "the steps to savings." These steps amount to a common-sense order and approach to ISO 9000 registration. Here are their main points.[4]

1 Learn as much about ISO 9000 as possible BEFORE hiring any outside help.
2 Select the ISO 9000 series that best suits your company.
3 Seek a registrar that meets your company's bureaucratic needs, as well as being accepted by overseas customers. Try to find a registrar with your industry background to meet the trend towards industry-specific guidelines.
4 Interview as many registrars as possible. Use these interviews as a means of learning more about individual registrars and more about the ISO 9000 process. Negotiate with your registrar. Generally, these are for-profit companies that must compete for your business.
5 Don't hire a registrar until you are ready to start your registration process. Make sure your contract includes all cancellation

and other clauses that will protect your financial interests as long as you choose to maintain ISO 9000 registration.

6 Organize your management and employees to work under an ISO 9000 team system.

7 Set up a data collection and documentation system BEFORE embarking on any documentation of procedures.

8 Seek advice, if necessary, from your registrar or outside qualified consultants when the need arises during the course of implementing the ISO 9000 standards in your field. Attempt an in-house preassessment audit before bringing in outsiders.

9 Pursue the ISO 9000 process, but perhaps forego the certificate. More and more companies are realizing that ISO 9000 certificates are not mandatory for survival in the international market. They are recognizing that the internal auditing methods ISO 9000 espouses can be helpful tools for creating a quality company. They are adopting ISO 9000 strategies without bothering to earn ISO 9000 registration.

10 Know that registration can pay for itself. The management at American Saw in East Longmeadow, Mass, is finding that ISO 9000 registration pays for itself. Employees are more involved in the process and more aware of company needs. The certificate has netted American Saw a number of new customers in the US and Europe.

SEVEN WAYS TO LAUNCH A *VALUE-ADDED ISO 9000*™ PROCESS[5]

Here are some steps to follow for the best coordination and efficient operation of an ISO 9000 documentation system.

1 Organize your management and employees into teams for the collection and processing of data.

2 The management advisory board or management team should establish a framework for data collection and processing based on the ISO 9000 requirements and the company's organization.

3 Uniform methods of data collection should be established up front, along with formats - graphs, tables, listings, and headings - under which to organize information.

4 Set up all formats in your computer network first, if such a network exists. In the absence of a computer system, establish typists who will sort and codify material employees gather.

5 Insure employees receive ample instructions in data collection before starting. Make sure those in charge of sorting data, formatting and producing your manual receive some instruction in editing and formatting.

6 Be flexible within the set formats you have established. Allow the process to dictate where additional topic areas may need to be added and others deleted.

7 Do not concern yourself with levels of ISO 9000 documentation until all data collection/processing systems are in place and tested.

With *Value-Added ISO 9000*™, employees may be asked to gather and process information totally unrelated to the ISO 9000 effort. It's up to management to be creative and determine what that information may be. At major companies like Philips Lighting, sales and logistics personnel now gather and exchange information for interdepartmental use. The uses of a *Value-Added ISO 9000*™ communication/documentation system are only limited by a company's imagination.

NOTES

1 Source: Robert H. Schaffer - Robert H. Schaffer & Associates, Quality Now!, *The Journal for Quality and Participation*, March 1989.

2 Source: Ten Steps to Total Service Quality, Lawrence Holpp, *The Journal for Quality and Participation*, March 1990.

3 Source: ISO Website

4 *ISO 9000 MADE EASY: A Cost-Saving Guide to Documentation and Registration* by Amy Zuckerman, formerly AMACOM Books and now published by A - Z International Associates, Amherst, MA, contains

many tips on making ISO 9000 work in the most cost-effective means possible.

5 Source: Amy Zuckerman, A–Z International Associates.
6 Source: Amy Zuckerman, "Did You Expect More Out of Your ISO 9000 Process? Adding Value to Your ISO 9000 Process," *The Journal for Quality and Participation*, January/February 1996.

Frequently Asked Questions (FAQs)

Q1: What is meant by quality?

A: See Chapter 2, Section: Defining "your" quality and Section: What is the most basic way to determine your quality requirements?

Q2: People keep talking about ISO 9000, what is it and what does it have to do with quality?

A: See Chapter 1, Section: What is ISO 9000 and why is it so important today and for the future? and Section: Three key reasons to consider ISO 9000.

Q3: How do I determine what my customers want in quality?

A: See Chapter 2, Section: What is the most basic way to determine your quality requirements?, Chapter 7, Section: Prudential Assurance Company, and Chapter 8, Section: Getting to what's important from the customers.

Q4: How did ISO 9000 get started and how has it changed?

A: See Chapter 3, Section: ISO 9000 and the "permanent" quality revolution.

Q5: Who has been doing really good work?

A: See Chapter 7, Section: Prudential Assurance Company and Section: Sundaram-Clayton of India wins Japan's 1999 Deming Prize.

Q6: Who do I look to for models?

A: See Chapter 7, Section: Three simple tools with big results and Section: Sundaram-Clayton of India wins Japan's 1999 Deming Prize, Chapter 8, Table 8.1: Crosby, Deming, and Juran compared, and Chapter 10, Section: Step two.

Q7: Where do I go for more information?

A: See Chapter 9.

Q8: Is there a way we can get off to a fast start?

A: See Chapter 10, Section: Jump starting your quality management system.

Q9: What about the people side of quality?

A: See Chapter 8, Section: The keys to the people side of quality.

Q10: What does the ISO say about starting a quality process?

A: See Chapter 10, Section: ISO's suggested steps for beginning a quality management system.

Index

Printed and bound in the UK by
CPI Antony Rowe, Eastbourne

Printed and bound by CPI Group (UK) Ltd, Croydon, CR0 4YY

09/06/2025

14686142-0001